The Thai Table

A CELEBRATION OF CULINARY TREASURES

Terry Tan

Marshall Cavendish Cuisine

Editor : Sylvy Soh
Designer : Lynn Chin Nyuk Ling
Photographer : Jambu Studio

Copyright © 2007 Marshall Cavendish International (Asia) Private Limited

Published by Marshall Cavendish Cuisine
An imprint of Marshall Cavendish International
1 New Industrial Road, Singapore 536196

Other Marshall Cavendish Offices:
Marshall Cavendish Ltd. 119 Wardour Street, London W1F 0UW, UK
• Marshall Cavendish Corporation. 99 White Plains Road, Tarrytown NY
10591-9001, USA • Marshall Cavendish International (Thailand) Co Ltd.
253 Asoke, 12th Flr, Sukhumvit 21 Road, Klongtoey Nua, Wattana, Bangkok
10110, Thailand • Marshall Cavendish (Malaysia) Sdn Bhd, Times Subang,
Lot 46, Subang Hi-Tech Industrial Park, Batu Tiga, 40000 Shah Alam,
Selangor Darul Ehsan, Malaysia

Marshall Cavendish is a trademark of Times Publishing Limited

National Library Board Singapore Cataloguing in Publication Data

Tan, Terry.
The Thai Table: a celebration of culinary treasures /- Terry Tan.
– Singapore :- Marshall Cavendish Cuisine,- c2007.
p. cm.
Includes index.
ISBN-13 : 978-981-261-442-1
ISBN-10 : 981-261-442-7

1. Cookery, Thai. I. Title.

TX724.5.T5
641.59593 -- dc22   OCN166246611

Printed in Singapore by KWF Printing Pte Ltd

Contents

Beginnings

Some twenty-five years ago, Thai restaurants in western cities were thinner on the ground than morning dew in summer. Malaysian and Indonesian cuisines—the closest to Thai, outside Indo-China, in spicy semantics and culinary evolution—had had earlier inroads, established in tandem with the demand for comfort food from many students of these two countries doing their academic grind in London, Sydney, Dublin and wherever. The spicy fragrance of lemon grass, galangal, kaffir lime leaves, chillies and a whole host of scented herbs, much loved by Thai chefs, were for centuries still seven-league boot leaps away.

As a cuisine, it was barely discernible and only manifest in very few family-run eateries in the major cities and towns in the western hemisphere. Australia probably had a head start because many Vietnamese and Thais found it more expedient, and nearer, to emigrate Down Under seeking fresh fields and invariably opening up little eating places. Backpackers from Down Under were also tripping all over Asia and having their taste buds utterly seduced by *satay*, *nasi goreng* and *tom yam* from Bali to Bangkok, from Singapore to Kuala Lumpur.

Thus, the love affair between the West and Thai cooking came to be flamed ever more so, spreading its subtle fire and exquisite culinary mien to London, New York, San Francisco and beyond. Punters became enamoured with the savoury richness of coconut milk, tangy lime leaves, piquant prawn (shrimp) paste, tongue-searing chillies, a plethora of heady herbs and pungent seasonings that were far removed from, and eminently more gustatory than, the European genre of meat and potatoes. Indian and Chinese eateries had been dominant for much longer but had also run their course in exotic and novelty value after more than half a century, compounded by the travesty of most restaurant and takeaway owners creating Anglo-Indian and unrecognisable Chinese hybrids that did neither cuisine any service. There was that awful commercial syndrome of 'meeting demand' which really said "let's give the *farangs* any old rubbish because they wouldn't know any different".

Thai consciousness was given its wake-up call in the mid 1980s and became positively assertive over those in places where there had been a twinkling of interest in things Thai. It was a culinary sea change that was to see a deluge of packaged, frozen and fresh Thai fruits, vegetables and spices in every corner of the globe. Thai cooking had become a buzzword that is still resounding across the world today.

5

Tom yam, green curry and *phad Thai* have become welcome intruders in western kitchens and homes, titillating the taste buds of many who hitherto knew little about Thailand beyond the Hollywood hype of *The King and I* genre, as have, to a lesser extent, Laotian and Kampuchean cuisine in European cities where people from Laos and Kampuchea had sought resettlement or refuge. As part of Indo-China, these two culinary disciplines bear many similarities to Thai, in some instances acting as springboard introductions to Thai.

There was an awakening of interest in this Asian region and trippers became ever more fascinated by these exotic realms, particularly the infamous sin city of Bangkok. This served to sharpen these taste buds even more, to the very knife-edge of culinary sophistication. Where tandoories and sweet and sours had previously held sway, the exquisite elements of Thai cuisine now eclipsed them.

The reasons for this remarkable shift in selective dining are bound with the semantics of the cuisine that has its roots in India dating back to 2000 BC, with many other influences from China, Malaysia and other neighbouring Indo-Chinese countries. The scenario has done an even more astonishing cartwheel lately where Thai elements are being interwoven into European cuisine, forging an ever more exquisite fusion plate. Peppered across this book are some delicious examples of these fusion dishes courtesy of some of the most august non-Thai chefs in the business.

Sanuk Thai cuisine

The region that embraced Myanmar (previously known as Burma), Vietnam, Kampuchea (now known as Kampuchea), Laos and Thailand had come to be collectively known as Indo-China, and part of the ancient Hindu Sri Vijaya Empire. Thai culture, language and religion are, as a result, inextricably bound with Hindu Buddhism. The cuisine naturally drew upon these evolutionary factors and it is, fundamentally, Indian in essence, but resplendently indigenous because of the cornucopia of spices, herbs, edible plants, fruits and seafood around the coastal regions.

The essence of Thai cuisine lies in the artful blend of fresh and dried herbs that are predominantly spicy with intriguing hints of tangy and heady aromatics. It is an exquisite bouquet fragrant with coriander, lemon grass, coconut, tamarind, galangal, chillies, sweet basil, ginger, garlic and shallots that underscore much of the cuisine's resplendent flavours. The keynote lies in the alchemy forged from these fresh herbs, usually ground into a paste and cooked in a little oil in tandem with coconut milk, tamarind juice and rich, traditional stocks. If there is a catchword for enjoying life among the Thais, be it food or other sybaritic pursuits, it is encapsulated in one pithy Thai expression–'*Sanuk*', which means to enjoy to the fullest extent.

Not surprisingly, given the country's historical roots, many Thai curries are Indian-style redolent with chillies, garlic, cardamom, cloves, cinnamon and onions that immeasurably complement the herby elements infused within some of the spicy blends. Still, Thai cuisine is unlike Indian cooking in the aspect that takes a large leaf from Hindu and Muslim religious tenets that eschew beef and pork respectively; as for the more esoteric Vegan disciplines that disallow garlic, onions and all animal matter, Thai cuisine knows few, if any religious boundaries.

Having spent the last 24 years in Britain and travelling the world for even longer in search of the most exciting viands, I have witnessed the ascension of Thai cuisine with much delight. It is a cuisine that is close to my heart, growing up within an extended family with any number of unexplained aunts who hailed from different Southeast Asian and Indo-Chinese countries. My father was dark-skinned and spoke mainly Indonesian and a little Chinese. We only knew that he had jumped a junk to seek his fortune in Singapore in the early 1900s. Of his antecedents, we knew little. My mother's maternal grandmother had a heritage that was part Chinese, part Malay and more than a soupçon of Thai bloodlines. We shared our rambling family house with some two dozen people during the Japanese war years. Many of my maternal relatives hailed from Penang and South Thailand, and I learned much from osmosis.

These were difficult post-war years with frequent evacuation of displaced families and our house seemed to have an endless stream of semi-permanent visitors. My earliest memories are of particularly glorious weekends when just about everyone would be marshalled to cook the family meals. Inevitably, I had the pungent task of grinding endless mortars of onions, chillies and eye-stinging pastes. We would often sit down some dozen people to lunch and dinner and each meal was a thrilling eclectic repast.

There would be curries rich with Indonesian spices, mouth-watering Thai style *satays*, salads and always, with many side dishes of sharp, limey flavours amid the briny bouquets of fish sauce and prawn (shrimp) pastes. It mattered little what they were called as we cared more about taste and flavour.

It was an extended family in the truest sense– maiden aunts baby-sitting, mother grinding spices, my sisters employed to kill, gut and clean chickens and my brothers and myself invariably given the messiest chores. Unconsciously, I was learning how to cook the best way that became embedded in my instincts, even from the tender age of 10. Thus, I became ever more adept at blending fresh herbs for green curry, tossing salads of the most exotic nature with green papaya, mango and banana flower buds. I learnt how to choose the best fish for specific dishes and acquired the artful skill of presenting them with panache.

Contrary to popular belief, making spice blends is not a fiddly, complicated chore, as long as you have access to the ingredients, which, thanks be, are today almost universally available. Not too long ago, lemon grass, galangal, screwpine (*toei*) leaves, coconut milk, limes, tamarind and kaffir lime leaves were virtually unheard of in the West. Today, television cooking shows fronted by non-Asians extol the flavours of these herbs and spices like they are native to the menus presented. *Tom yam*, Massaman curry and *phad Thai* have been fiercely embraced by those enamoured of the cuisine.

The T'ai and Thais

If there is one country that lends itself to myriad imageries, it is Thailand. The most popular one being of gilded temples and glorious palaces, the endless, snaking *klongs* or waterways that still attract hordes of tourists soaking up the thrilling ambience of the floating markets; of sun-kissed beaches and pristine white sands; exotic hill tribes and their traditional cultures and, of course, the incredible, peripatetic metropolis that is Bangkok. Yet, the essence of Thailand is more than a sum of these parts. Thai cuisine is inextricably interwoven with the culture, a near mystical mix of fragrant flavours and intriguing history that has few peers.

Thailand is about the size of continental France and encompasses a bewildering range of topography. To the north are soaring mountains that mark the borders of Myanmar and Laos, some rising to more than 2,500 metres ($1^1/_2$ miles). The valleys that nestle between these ranges are lush and verdant, with much of their original teak forests denuded to satisfy the global taste for teak furniture.

Historical records show that the Thais were by no means the first settlers here. Paleolithic Age archeological evidence that date back some half a million years ago, have been found in caves near the border of Myanmar. Fossils of water chestnuts, squashes and cucumber have been found here that date back to 9000 BC.

Indian traders much later had also established ports along the southern peninsula, bringing with them not only Buddhism but also culinary elements. At around the same time, Mon tribesmen from the mountains arrived to settle in the Chao Phraya Valley and to cultivate rice. They were eventually overthrown by the pugnacious Khmers, whose empire once stretched over most of Thailand.

Who then were the ethnic Thais? Some 75 per cent of citizens were descended from a broad ethnic and linguistic group called the T'ai, in what is now southern China. Today, some 12 per cent of Thai people are of Chinese descent, most hailing originally from the provinces of Fujian and Guangzhou and the island of Hainan. It is inevitable that Thai cuisine has absorbed elements, however subtle, from each of these cuisines, known as *ahaan chin* or Chinese cooking. In the far north lives a large community of Chinese Muslims, the Hui people who had emigrated from Yunnan province in the late 19th century. They still retain much of their traditional culinary culture, and pork, which is eschewed by Islam, does not figure in their menus.

Added to this is a sprinkling of ethnic Malays, also largely Muslim, concentrated mainly in the southern provinces. Making up the remainder are small communities of non Thai-speaking Vietnamese, Khmer, Mon tribe people, Sakai aborigines, the nomadic Moken or sea gypsies as they are better known, Htin, Mabri, Khamu and other hill tribes. The earliest groups had settled in the far north forming a loose federation of city-states centred around what is now Chiang Mai. By the middle of the 13th century, there were such numbers of them that they were able to rout the Khmer overlords and establish a kingdom of their own.

The Dawning of the Kingdom

This was the kingdom of Sukothai, which means Dawn of Happiness in the ancient Pali-Sanskrit language. The Sukothai kingdom was to last only two centuries but in that time, under the leadership of King Ramkhamhaeng, the Thai alphabet was devised, many works of Buddhist art were created and an indigenous Thai culture emerged to last until today.

Ayutthaya, the next capital built around 1350 on the Chao Phraya River, thrived for the next four centuries. The Thai culture was to be enriched by its first contact with Europe and trade flourished with other Asian countries. By the 18th century, Ayutthaya had fallen to the marauding Burmese army but scarcely 15 years later, they were beaten back by the Thai army and a new capital was established further south, at Thonburi.

In 1782, a charismatic young military leader, King Rama I founded the present Chakri Dynasty and moved the capital across the Chao Phraya River to what is now Bangkok or the official Thai name of *Krung Thep*. He built many palaces, carved out intricate canals that served as riverine streets and also built the stunning Temple of the Emerald Buddha, richly reflective of those in Ayutthaya. This reverent statue carved out of a single piece of green jasper or jadeite, is the most sacred icon in the country.

The temple still stands today, as a sparkling and unblemished beacon of Thai Buddhist culture.

Though the kingdom's independence was maintained, if somewhat precariously, there was no stemming the flow of European traders and migrants from southern China. By the late 19th century, Bangkok was well on its way to becoming a modern metropolis. The rural scenario was, and still is, a different thing altogether. Villagers still cling to their ancient traditions and are able to resist modern influences (apart from the intrusive television) as many of their settlements were, and still are, relatively isolated.

Because of this, traditional cooking has kept most of its heritage. A case in point is Bangkok; while offering a facade that is thoroughly sassy and modern, many chefs have their hearts in the rural hinterland and their cooking speaks resonantly of this.

The Essence of Thai Food

Whether searing hot or subtly mild, the guiding principle in Thai cooking is harmony. Fundamentally, it is an aromatic marriage of centuries-old Eastern and Western influences, the chief characteristics being who cooks it, for whom it is cooked, for what occasion and where it is cooked. To the cook, preparing Thai dishes is extremely personal; from how they are refined for particular tastes, befit a special function or festival, and where they originate. With its roots in a waterborne lifestyle, aquatic animals, plants and herbs are all major ingredients. Once you fathom the semantics of balance, the compatibility of ingredients and the many subtleties that underscore each dish, the rest is a matter of practice to make perfect.

A Fragrant Beginning

Although little about early Sukothai cuisine has been chronicled, we know that much of Thailand's early culinary history rested on rice and seafood. Fruits also featured prominently not only as sweet afters, but were frequently included in savoury dishes, if not carved for spectacular effect as dressage. Despite the fact that Thai cuisine is characterised by the fiery chilli pod indigenous to South America, it actually did not appear until the late 16th century when it was brought east by Europeans. The Portuguese were already trading with Thailand and it is also possible that the chilli came by way of Malacca and India. The former, a seaport along the Malaysian west coast, was already a Portuguese enclave.

As observed by one French diplomatic visitor Simon de la Loubere of the 17th century:

"The Siamese people make very good meals with a pound of rice a day, with a little dry or salt fish. They serve plain sauce with some spices, garlic and perhaps a sweet herb."

Loubere also made reference to the early use of a pungent salted fish called "kepi". Today, we know that the ubiquitous prawn (shrimp) paste so fundamental to Thai curries is called "*kapi*".

As the sands of time trickled on, Thai cooking became more complex, relying much on a blend of fermented prawn paste (*kapi*), lemon grass, galangal, ginger, lime leaves, spicy basil, chilli, cloves, nutmeg, garlic, onions and ginger. Cloves and nutmeg had come from trade with the East Indies and the Chinese, Malay and Indian residents in Ayutthaya by the mid-16th century already knew about and used these spices liberally. The many Thai sweet desserts based on egg and sugar were also inspired by many a Portuguese pastry concoction.

Many Westerners today are familiar with the basics of Thai cuisine, an unchanging trail through green curry, *tom yam*, *satay*, red curry and pineapple rice. Visit Thailand to embark on a provincial journey, and you will be amazed by the sheer diversity of cooking styles and dishes. In many cases, the differences between, say a Bangkok curry and a Chiang Mai version are so subtle, it would take an expert to fully appreciate.

Table Culture

It is often assumed that Thais use chopsticks as often as the Chinese. In truth, the Thai dining table rarely features them and a typical place setting would be a large dinner plate, fork and spoon and perhaps a side bowl and porcelain spoon for soup. Chopsticks are employed only when soupy noodles are served. Every meal is communal wherein all the dishes are served at the same time and diners help themselves from each plate or bowl of curries, stir-fried dishes or side dips. In many rural pockets, Thais still eat with their fingers, using various leaves and rice crackers as makeshift spoons.

Regional Flavours

Given that the country is about the size of France, one would expect a mirror of regional culinary differences. Indeed, there are differences to be found, between the main zones of central, northern, northeastern and southern Thailand. Not only does the Thai topography differ greatly between all the compass points, but so do the people and food as well. In history, Thai kingdoms were often subjugated by neighbouring powers, a factor that has largely influenced the culinary evolution. Today, the four regional cuisines are largely recognised as distinctive schools.

Central Thailand

This is a region of cornucopian largesse, a silt-rich rice bowl with many of the rivers flowing southward into the Central Plain, resulting in an enormous delta with the mighty Menam Chao Phraya–the name means River of Kings–in dominance. Apart from rice, the region also supports a delicious pastiche of sugar cane, tapioca and a forest of fruits like mangoes, mangosteens, durians, rambutans, jackfruit, longan, limes, bananas and pomelos to name but just a few.

Such largesse naturally became a magnet to many Thais and the population is the densest of all the regions. There is a significant number of Mon people who are believed to be among the earliest settlers here, and the integration has been so that it is hard to tell them apart from the Thais, as most speak the standard Central Thai dialect.

But it is the cuisine that mesmerises most and is considered to be the classic form enriched by a bewildering range of spices, herbs and products from all corners of the land. One cannot help but draw an analogy from the Parisian style of cooking. From the south comes coconuts that not only provide liquid sustenance, but the all-important coconut milk for curries. What typifies the cooking here are *gaeng phet* (hot curries), the quintessential *gaeng khiew wan* (green curry) and the tangy and savoury coconut *tom kha* soup. Nor are the husks and shells ignored; the former being recycled into mattress stuffing, the shells transformed into a range of utensils like ladles, spoons, bowls and sundry containers.

Sweet basil that has a heady scent of aniseed and mint go into just about every curry, often given an irresistible crunch with bamboo shoots from the north. It has a close cousin in what is loosely termed Vietnamese coriander called *pak chi lao* also known as laksa leaf in the south and in Malaysia. Seafood dishes like *hor mog thalay* reflect southern briny produce, also spiced with turmeric, chillies, ginger, shallots and coconut milk. The catchall term for the cuisine of this region is '*ahaan phaak klaang*', that is also influenced by many Chinese characteristics especially in dishes like *phad Thai* (fried rice noodles) and mild soups (*gaeng chud*).

The Chinese are in general not overly fond of heavily spiced dishes and have infused many of the dishes with their favourite ingredients like tofu, soy sauce and oyster sauce as evidenced in stir-fried vegetarian concoctions. Central Thailand cuisine echoes that of Sichuan, wherein hot, sweet, sour and bitter flavours are combined brilliantly, breaking all the rules and getting away with it.

I have a penchant for one of Central Thailand's most ravishing dishes, *kway teow reau*, literally "boat noodles", that one is hard put to resist. Is it Chinese or Thai? A bit of both really, with broad, flat noodles that are a staple of the Teochew people of Swatow in China, being cooked in a rich broth of beef. Believed to have been first cooked and sold by the boat people who plied the canals of Rangsit, it has become ubiquitous throughout the region.

Another dish that does not often make a show in restaurants today is the esoteric *khao laam*. This is glutinous (sticky) rice cooked in coconut milk in a hollow bamboo joint that is a staple of the village people in Nakhon Pathom, some 97 km (60 miles) north of Bangkok, where the Phra Pathom Chedi, the largest Buddhist temple in the world is located.

West of Bangkok, in the Kanchanaburi Province, the Mon people whip up an intoxicating range of curries that are invariably served heaped on a plate of steaming jasmine rice. This is known as *khao gaeng* of which there are innumerable mixes, with chicken, seafood, beef, pork and vegetables, often all on the same plate!

Along the Chanthaburi River, largely a Vietnamese enclave, you'll find a delicious range of rice noodle dishes all swimming in broths hearty with beef stock and seafood, topped with mint, basil and fiery Thai bird's eye chillies. They are richly reminiscent of the national Vietnamese *pho*–beef noodles that earmark the cuisine. In Phetburi, south of Bangkok, your taste buds will be sweetened with an ingenious dessert called *khanom maw gaeng*–baked custard with mung bean purée, eggs, coconut milk and tons of sugar.

In the coastal town of Hua Hin, seafood is king, naturally. Catfish, cotton fish, mackerel, snapper and other tropical warm water denizens too numerous to mention, end up in spicy dishes crunchy with green mangoes, chillies and papaya.

Northern Thailand

Along the common borders of Myanmar and Laos in the mountainous north, the cuisine resounds with delicious echoes of the distinctive characteristics in the region's much-loved handicrafts like basketry and rustic, woven cotton apparel and accessories. Plain umbrellas become kaleidoscopes of jewel-like colours of pastoral and floral scenes. Vibrant colour and heady fragrances permeate the very air of these villages. The terrain has relatively few lowland areas for cultivation, but it is nevertheless a fount of ingenious cooking that draws from the harvest of a cooler climate.

The loose federation that grew from the group of small city-states came to be known as Lanna, with Chiang Mai as the principal city. The cuisine is collectively known as *ahaan neau* (northern Thai cuisine) that features many vegetables grown on hilly slopes. The splendidly tart, hot and savoury salad of green papaya shreds, chillies, beans, dried prawns (shrimp) and lime juice called *som tam*

hails from here. Even when *lanna*–the word is a singular description meaning "a million rice fields" came under the administrative control of Bangkok, it remained relatively remote from the rest of the country until 1921 when the first railway link was established between north and south.

But it is this very isolation that allowed North Thailand to retain and develop its own culture and language. The Thai spoken here is as different to that of the South as Italian is from Spanish. North Thailand is as known for its distinctive cuisine as its exquisite craft of lacquer, silver and carved wood *objet d'art*.

Curiously, although northerners are fond of glutinous rice, they tend to regard it more as an in-between meal snack rather than a staple as it is regarded in the northeast region of Isaan. Many indigenous roots and vegetables, rarely seen outside Thailand, are used liberally. There is a fondness for bitter flavours, as in *makheau prao*, a small aubergine that has unforgiving bitterness. Even bamboo shoots are pickled to within an inch of tart bitterness that go into sour curries and soups.

Banana plant hearts and green jackfruit are treated with near reverence, the former echoing a Burmese classic and of course, there is the spicy staple of sausages. Most are made with ground pork and spiced with chillies, lemon grass and lime leaves. Some can be of acquired tastes, as in *naem maw*, a blend of raw ground pork, sticky rice, salt, garlic and chillies that is wrapped with banana leaf, left for a few days to pickle and eaten uncooked.

Typical of this region is *nahm prik orng*, an unguent dip of ground, dried red chillies, ground pork, tomatoes, lemon grass, lime juice and fish sauce; *naam prik num* of green chillies, roasted aubergine and other fresh green herbs eaten with fried pork skin. Most pungent of all is *nahm prik nahm puu*, a rich condiment made from ground field crab cooked in its own juices and blended with shallots, garlic and chillies.

It is in the north that noodle dishes come into their own, the area being a crossroad of cultures from the ethnic mix of Yunnan, Shan and Burmese peoples. In Chiang Mai, you couldn't move a few metres without coming upon a noodle vendor offering *khao soi*–egg noodles with chicken or beef curry. A similar dish in Myanmar is called *hkauk swe* and Yunnanese Muslims still run eating places in Chiang Mai that offer this dish. It has a close Singapore cousin called *laksa* that is spiked with the aforementioned Vietnamese coriander.

Another noodle worthy of note is *woon sien* (translucent vermicelli made from mung bean flour that is resoundingly Chinese) that ends up in numerous dishes like *gaeng phak waan* (soup with greens), *gaeng yuak* (banana heart curry) and *phad woon sen* (fried noodles with pickled sausage and eggs.)

The Khan Tohk Heritage

The term refers to the serving of many small dishes (*khan*) on a small trestle or low table (*tohk*) that evolved from communal meals. Although the mode still persists in many homes, *khan tohk*, originally perceived as a diplomatic gesture, is today reserved for special occasions when there are honoured guests. As a cultural showcase, many travel agents and hotels in the 1980s began organising *khan tohk* evenings of fine food and entertainment. You can still enjoy such an evening, but do not expect a truly authentic presentation given its touristy *raison d'etre*.

North east Thailand

Usually referred to as Isaan, this region is dominated by the massive Khorat Plateau that rises to some 300 metres ($^1/_5$ mile) in the Central Plain. It has had a long history, with 4000-year-old Bronze Age artifacts unearthed in Ban Chiang. The people are called *khon Isaan* and the cuisine *ahaan Isaan*. The root word comes from *Isana*, a Sanskrit name that means "flowing with wealth". Southerners once looked upon Isaan cuisine as unsophisticated and even weird, but others say this is less of a geographical nature than one of social prejudice as the region is one of the poorest in Thailand, its name something of a paradox. Not known for diffidence in culinary matters, Isaan folk would not bat an eyelid when eating grasshoppers, ants, snails and other esoterics even the most adventurous Thai taste buds would curl up at. Possibly, this is where the 'weird' handle comes in.

Red ant larvae, water beetles, geckos and other creepy, crawly, slithery creatures are eaten with gusto by the locals. Some geckos are even raised commercially today, so there are no fears about upsetting conservationists. A common tongue-in-cheek comment is that in Thailand, there are far fewer geckos in the country today as the Isaan people have eaten most of them!

The culture reflects strong Lao and Khmer influences with many Khmer monuments still standing testimony to this evolution. Along the Mekong River still stand many Lao temples, including the sacred Wat Phra That Phanom. Many *khon Isaan* still speak a mixture of Thai and Lao, not surprisingly, since there are more people of Lao heritage here than in Laos!

Isaan food has found many aficionados in the south and even worldwide. Isaan chefs have a unique gift in transforming the humblest viands into magnificent dishes worthy of royal endorsement. *Som tam*, *gai yang* and *khao niaw* (papaya salad, grilled spiced chicken and glutinous rice) are the holy trinity of Isaan cuisine. *Gai yang* translates to joints of chicken marinated with garlic purée, coriander root, pepper and fish sauce before being charcoal-grilled. All are served with *khao niaw*.

Hor mog consists of a combination of simple river fish, spices and coconut milk, steamed or grilled in banana leaves. It is now a dish entrenched in the best of Thai restaurants around the world. *Pla duk*, a member of the catfish family, is an almost mythical (but real) creature that looks like it came out of some Jurassic swamp. It is so large, it can come in at 4 metres (157 inches) and weigh some 300 kg (660 lb). For the more adventurous, *laab dip* is a kind of sausage with chopped pork and roasted rice powder. As a generic, *laab* turns up in the most enticing guises–with beef or fish and sometimes even raw. If sweetening is needed, *naam maprao* (coconut sugar) is always the agent.

Beef, or rather buffalo, and venison are often marinated and grilled to be served with pungent dips of mint, onion, chillies, garlic and lime juice. Northeasterners have a penchant for chillies far greater than that of any other Thais. But whatever is served, sticky rice is the mainstay, either rolled into balls or served in small rattan baskets.

Isaan soups (*toms*) resemble Central Thai offerings; the range of '*toms*', usually perfumed with lemon grass, galangal, spring onions, lime leaves and chillies. No Isaan meal is complete without one *tom* or another–as in *tom wua* (with beef tripe and liver) and *tom fak* (with green marrow).

Southern Thailand

This covers the narrow neck of Thailand that consists of flat plains along both coasts, narrowing down at the Isthmus of Kra and at it widest point, embraces 14 provinces. The topography is typically flat with abundant rainforests and the culture has remained largely distinct from the rest of the country. Historically, it had close ties with Indonesia, in particular the ancient Sri Vijaya Empire that once held court over most of what are today Southern Thailand, Malaysia and the Indonesian Archipelago. Thus, a Malay-Indonesian culture still marks the ethnicity, religion and cuisine of the *Thai pak tai* (Southern Thais).

Their apparel, architectural and culinary elements are unique. Islam is the prevalent religion here, particularly in the four southern provinces bordering Malaysia. In Satun, some 80 per cent of the population are Muslims and throughout the region, there are only some dozen Buddhist temples compared to more than 125 Islamic mosques. The cities are largely populated by Chinese and some Sakai aboriginals.

I recall my father taking my two brothers and myself to a Sakai settlement near the southern town of Songkhla. The Sakai leader was a white-haired woman of indeterminate age, but it was not her mien that frightened us. It was the fact that she had, slung on the belt that held up her grimy cotton sarong, a fearsome *parang* (Malaysian scimitar). Our translator and bodyguard, armed with a sub-machine gun, told us that she had in fact decapitated a few communist interlopers during the Post War years when they were opposing Japanese occupation. Needless to say, we declined the invitation to stay in her tree hut.

Southern Thai cooks are amazingly adept at improvising and as such, the range of curries is mouth-wateringly wide. *Pla khluk kha-min* translates to fish marinated with fresh turmeric, garlic and salt. *Khao yam* is an aromatic blend of dry, cooked rice with grated coconut, bean sprouts, lime leaves, lemon grass and dried prawns (shrimps) that echo the Malaysian staple of *nasi ulam* (rice with jungle herbs). *Mu daeng* is barbecued pork that takes a large leaf from the Cantonese staple of *char siew* (roast red pork) and not surprisingly, *roti* is eaten widely. The very word means "bread" in the Indian dialect and derives from the Indian *paratha*, a round, flat bread served with mutton curry.

Paak thong koh is a literal translation of the Cantonese steamed white bread often eaten as a sweet snack. The Chinese-Thais and Thai Muslims of Phang-Nga, Krabi and Phuket eat *khao mok khai*, a rice and chicken dish cooked with rich Indian spices that resembles the Kashmiri *biryani*.

Bangkok

Once known as Bang Makok on account of the many groves of the native Ma-Kawk tree, the city, officially also known as Krung Thep, is home to some 10 per cent of Thailand's population. The name Bangkok persisted among foreign traders and is still preferred by most outside the kingdom. As a tourist hotspot, it continues to lure millions to its peripatetic mix of carnal, spiritual and entrepreneurial activities. As a city that seems to have dragged itself from the Middle Ages to the 21st century in the blink of an eye, it is a fascinating melange of mind-boggling contradictions. At once a megalopolis of futuristic mien and the seat of ancient Thai culture, it begs to be devoured by all the senses.

It also brings together all the culinary styles of the kingdom, like Central Thai cooking, which dominates cuisine style and flavour, but with many subtle Mon and Chinese influences. *Gaeng phed yang* is a perfect marriage of Cantonese roast duck, Thai spices and coconut milk. Although shopping malls and food courts contain the inevitable fast food outlets, you are never more than a short stroll away from some coffee shop, hawker centre or restaurant that offer genuine Thai dishes. The variety is nothing short of astounding, especially in the side roads leading off Silom and Sukhumvit roads downtown.

Thai Curries

There is ample justification for singling out Thai curries (*gaeng*) for special mention. To begin with, the range is bewildering and wherever you go, to homes, villages, towns, cities and regions, there are curries indigenous to each. Thais have a heartfelt pride for their spicy concoctions that rest on many factors: availability of ingredients, seasonal produce, regional semantics, techniques, personal tastes and local traditions.

The *gaeng* that we are now becoming more familiar with is a far distant trumpet call from what is generally perceived as curry in the West. Simple or complex, the fundamentals of a Thai curry are defined by three elements: spices, the method of cooking and the main ingredients of meat, poultry, seafood or vegetables. *Gaeng ped* refers to a highly seasoned and thick liquid. *Gaeng chud* in contrast refers to one that is bland and not much more substantial than a soup.

What is important in a good Thai curry is that no particular single flavour should overshadow another, the whole, a harmonious blend. Experienced Thai curry chefs know instinctively what ingredients are compatible and which mix produces the most cohesive results.

They have had a good head start as curries have evolved and been refined over centuries (See chapter on Curries, Dips and Pastes).

Floating Markets

Undeniably one of the most enchanting experiences in Bangkok, the *talaat naam* has become an institution. In common parlance, this means water market. A more universally recognised name is "floating market". Floating markets take place in the early dawn hours on the canals of Central Thailand. Everything from fruits to noodles, carved elephants to umbrellas, Coke and ice cream are hawked amid a raucous atmosphere that is irresistible to shutterbugs. For me, it is the epitome of Thai eating experience to be served a steaming hot bowl of beef noodles from a bobbing boat, to be eaten while I am trying to strike a stable balance in another bobbing boat. Head for the canals of Ratchaburi, Samut Sakhon and Samut Songkhram, provinces southwest of Bangkok and other points along the hundreds of kilometres of waterways surrounding the city.

Street Food

The itinerant street hawkers of Thailand are an integral element in the lives of Thais. It is a heritage that demands more respect than one would accord it. It seems every city street, market square, roadside drive-in, crumbling fortification wall and even railway platform function like round-the-clock food fairs; with mobile *satay* vendors heating up the already humid atmosphere with their charcoal braziers; noodle stalls on makeshift carts that are enchanting meals-on-wheels and children hawking pieces of anything edible from sugar cane joints to homemade banana fritters.

Less than a century ago, this mode of food vending characterised almost all Asian towns and villages wherein people did not go looking for food as it came to them. The sub-culture that evolved around the *rot khen* (vendor cart) has become so entrenched, it is difficult to imagine Thailand without it. Not necessarily a different cuisine as such, these foods have evolved mainly from the need for many to eke out a living. Most are simple, rustic dishes that have become virtual classics in the genre.

There does not seem to be a fine line between what is a snack and what is a meal, given that Thais eat constantly. Taste is all, and who would turn down such smooth, savoury *johk*, also known as congee and derived from the Cantonese rice porridge that is a velvety, savoury concoction of broken rice cooked with pork, chicken or fish and spiced up with ginger and pepper?

Other typical dishes are *satay* (skewers of spiced meat grilled and served with a spicy sauce rich with ground peanuts), chicken wrapped in screwpine (*toei*) leaf, dumplings, jumbo prawns in batter, tantalising soups, fragrant fish cakes and salads oozing with the combined essences of lemon grass, ginger, chillies and lime. In fact, come any hour and especially after sundown, the very air of Bangkok, Chiang Mai and other suburban and urban areas with any sizeable community, is perfumed with the mingled scents of sharp citrus tang, fried onions, pungent garlic, fragrant coriander and eye-stinging chillies.

Over the past three decades in which I have made many visits to Thailand, I never fail to make a beeline for the food centre known as Maboonkong, now abbreviated to MBK, like some latter fast food joint. A solid block is devoted to six air-conditioned floors with several given over to food, glorious food. And what an offering from this salubrious extension of

street stalls within a comfortable and absolutely clean environment that still serves delicious and incredibly inexpensive dishes from all over the country.

Braised goose, noodles of every hue, *satays*, chicken in a dozen different Thai guises, salads, stir-fries and other traditional Thai dishes covering the spectrum of mild, savoury, hot and tongue-searing can be had for less than a song. What is most interesting about the place that locals flock to daily is the mode of purchasing. You buy coupons for what you order at the stalls, then redeem any unused value. Any *tuk-tuk* and taxi driver will take you right to the doorstep.

Oodles of Noodles

But it is noodles that truly typify street food—strands made from wheat, rice and other flours of every imaginable hue, crunch and flavour. Fried with egg, in soup, chillied or left innocent of all but a handful of bean sprouts, noodles are hawked from dusk to dawn like an endless taste parade. Many have become celebrated in their own right, family recipe secrets that no amount of cash would entice the vendors to part with them. It is not uncommon for even the most affluent Thais in their limos and flashy cars to drive hundreds of kilometres in search of their favourite noodle stall.

Other hawker stalls are an exotic picture of delicious promise; whole octopus trailing their tentacles almost down to street level are grilled and hacked into serving portions; baby chickens and even birds are skewered on bamboo sticks and cooked on glowing embers; aromatic salads tossed in huge terracotta mortars—these and more make up the endless pastiche that is Thai street food.

Palace Cooking

One must not forget that even though Thai cooking in general remains fairly close to the ground, affordable and common to most, there is another more refined level. It has always prevailed in royal and aristocratic echelons, most often referred to as Palace Cooking or Royal Cuisine. Obviously, the Thai royal households then or now, could afford a brigade of first class chefs and other kitchen help. It was from here that the art of fruit and vegetable carving truly blossomed.

In the early years of this century, the Thai Royal Palace was described as the 'Inside' where, at its peak there was a population of some 3,000. Much misunderstood by observers and historians as a hotbed of polygamy–witness the English teacher Anna Leon Owens who referred to it as a "harem" –the truth is far removed from the Western concept of fantasy.

Protocol demanded that women's quarters were segregated from men's in the Royal Palace and many aristocratic families sent their daughters there for grooming in preparation for their future lives. There, they were not only taught how to behave regally and to observe all the subtle nuances of royal behaviour, but also to learn all the exquisite aspects of *cuisinarte* that would stand them in brilliant stead when royal swains came a-wooing.

By the era of the Rattanakosin, also known as the Bangkok period, Thai cuisine as we know it today, was firmly established throughout the land. According to some 19th century accounts, the favourite Thai fish seasoning called *nam prik* was a staple. One English visitor waxed positively lyrical about a sauce that uses this seasoning and that we know today as a made condiment called *nam prik orng*. He described it with mouth-watering prose: *"a small quantity of red pepper is bruised in a mortar, to which is added shrimp paste, black pepper, garlic and onions. A small quantity of brine and citrus juice is added together with ginger and tamarind."*

It was more of an exclusive finishing school where daughters of blue bloods and other minor aristocracy learned many delicate arts like floral decoration, threading fragrant flowers into wreaths and laurels and making exquisite miniature vegetables and fruits with mung bean paste and coconut milk called *loop choop*. Most of all, they learnt how to cook the finest dishes that required many hours of painstaking preparation.

Under their milk-white hands, watermelons, mangoes, pumpkins, chillies and root vegetables would be transformed into magnificently realistic flowers and other heraldic designs. Royal polygamy ended under the reign of King Rama VI, but there were a few women still in residence as late as 1960. They soon left this rarified atmosphere and entered another less protective world outside. Fortunately, palace cooking did not vanish and has survived through the descendants of the royal women and today, resuscitated by the legion of Thai chefs around the world and rediscovered by Thai food enthusiasts from Sydney to Singapore, from London to Los Angeles and beyond.

Rice Culture

Rice is more than a staple plateful to Thai culinary culture. Indeed, the very tenet of all Southeast Asian and Indo-Chinese cultures rests on this grain, be it ever so humble. Rice culture had actually arrived with the earliest settlers to Thailand, long before the Thai people made it their permanent home. These settlers had carved out a vast complex of paddy fields watered by a remarkably intricate system of rivers, canals and impounded reservoirs.

Several centuries before Christianity, kingdoms and empires in the region were already highly organised and sophisticated, and their power seemed to rest on the very cultivation of rice. For one thing, most of these lands are located in the extremely fertile deltas of the rivers Mekong and Menam Chao Phraya and the Irrawaddy and Red rivers.

As a crop growing in these flood plains and waterlogged deltas, the modus operandi for nurturing of rice is the drainage of water. Most of the canals that date back thousand of years were built just for this purpose.

By about 600 BC, rice was already a primary crop in most of Indo-China including Thailand, the other countries that evolved from centuries of Indo-Chinese trade and intermarriages being Myanmar, Vietnam, Kampuchea and Laos. In some cases, especially in the Philippines, rice culture stretches back some 4,000 years. Thailand remains one of the biggest importers of rice and ranks fifth among global producers.

Thai rice growers were wont to subscribe to many traditional beliefs. They resolutely would not plough their fields until the king of Thailand had ploughed a ceremonial furrow to appease the appropriate deities, one of whom is Mae Thorani, regarded by Buddhists as the Goddess of Vegetation. The farmers would also offer gifts of food, flowers and prayers as an act that purportedly flattered the rice buds so they would fatten. When the grains are fully ripened, more thanks are offered to Mae Phosop or the Rice Mother.

Farmers' wives would craft rice dolls from dried stalks of the paddy plant, treating them like royalty and calling the soul of the rice to inhabit the dolls. Barbie, despite her Hollywood wardrobe, has nothing on her Thai counterparts for *chutzpah*! These are then installed in the granary with sombre ceremony to ensure another season of plenty. Many of these rituals, however, have been relegated to the back burner of history today, not because of modern disbelief, but because modern farming methods can positively ensure bumper harvests.

What is important is the fact that all Thais—indeed all Asians—hold rice with absolute reverence. It is the perfect foil and cushion for the country's delectable curries, sensuous salads, sauces and stir-fries. So dependent on rice were the early Thais that they never embarked on any migratory journey without bags of the grain. It was as much for sustenance as it was for spiritual comfort, and it shaped the destiny of the country to become the rice bowl of Asia. It is understandable that the term for "eat" in Thai is "*khin khao*" literally meaning "to consume rice". The common greeting when people meet reflects this even more strongly, the salutation in translation being "have you eaten rice?"

Anyone visiting Thailand today, especially as they approach by air, will notice that the sensuous curves of old rice field boundaries carved millennia ago, have been replaced by linear arrangements that are the result of mechanisation.

Northerners go through tons of glutinous rice or sticky rice, as it is more popularly known. During festive occasions and in some families, the mode of eating this rice is still to form them into small balls to be dipped in a selection of pungent and spicy dips. In earlier times, this was about all that was eaten. Actually the name of glutinous rice is something of a misnomer as it purports to the grain containing gluten. Rice does not contains any gluten. The stickiness comes from the presence of starch. Almost all glutinous rice varieties are short grain and because of their structure, adhere together much better. Unlike the south where glutinous rice is usually relegated to after dinner desserts–as in mango and glutinous rice–northerners eat it at every meal every day.

A Typical Thai Meal

The ideal Thai meal is, and has been for centuries, built around rice and dishes, forging a harmonious blend of the spicy, the subtle, the sweet and the sour; the sum being more mouthwatering than the parts. Every meal is meant to be equally endearing to the eye, nose and palate. Thus most meals, however simple or grand would have a clear soup, a fish or shellfish dish, a fried dish of meat or poultry, a hot salad, a curry of some kind and a variety of sharp, pungent, sour or sweet dips.

While snacks and finger foods proliferate in Thailand, there is an absence of starters and appetisers in a typical meal. The ones profiled in this book are really a token gesture to the Western mode of dining and not from any classical culinary tenet. Small bites preceding a meal are in reality "outside the meal". All dishes are served at once and every meal is communal. There is an old Chinese saying: "every mouthful is a new symphony". There is usually a nice balance of something crisp, something sour, spicy, tangy and so on.

There is not much by way of accompanying drinks in a Thai meal, water being the general preference across the country. In fact, it used to be considered improper to drink during a meal and light soups were served to refresh the palate between mouthfuls. Contemporary mores are less cognizant of this ancient etiquette and Thais today will drink whatever they fancy, usually local beer and increasingly, wine. The choice of which wine goes with what dish is a highly subjective matter, the grape having arrived only recently. Who is to say that a fiery curry may not be washed down with a Beaujolais? Or that a well-chilled Chardonnay cannot do justice to a mango dessert?

Given a choice, most Thais will stick to what they are most familiar with–fruit juices. And these are very much embedded within the culinary culture. But not for them the boring bottled or canned stuff; the tropical fruit basket of Thailand being a veritable orchard of sweet, fragrant and honeyed flavours. Rambutans, mangoes, mangosteens, jackfruit, starfruit, papayas and melons of every hue are whirled and liquidised to be served with crushed ice. It is a feature of street food and long may it last.

Sweet Afters

As desserts go, the range of Thai sweets is neither exhaustingly extensive nor an integral part of family meals. It is not like the entrenched western tradition to finish a meal with a 'pudding', to paraphrase this catch-all word in western dining parlance. Indeed in the north, what passes for a dessert after a meal of spicy dishes is more often than not steamed glutinous rice liberally sprinkled with palm sugar. It is rustic, but the distinctive fragrance of palm sugar when married with rice forges a remarkable alchemy.

In fact, throughout Asia, sweet bites are the stuff of anytime snacks. Dairy produce like milk and cream simply do not exist within the Asian spectrum of cooking and there is not much by way of pre-prepared mixes. The basis of most Thai desserts comes from a blend of rice flour, coconut milk and palm sugar. If there is one product that should typify Thai desserts, it is this last ingredient.

Nonetheless, these concoctions, often perfumed with screwpine (*toei*) leaf or rose water, constitute an important place in Thai homes, especially in royal households where kitchens were firmly divided into sweet and savoury departments. Dessert chefs did nothing else but whip up delectable concoctions and often spent years training for the job. Offerings were even made to the Lord Buddha in their honour!

Cooking and Eating Fruits

It may seem strange at first that fruits should be accorded a cooking function, but this mode is no stranger to Mediterranean cuisine for instance, as dates, apricots and apples have always been used in savoury dishes. Since Thailand abounds with a plethora of fruits, many end up in main course dishes. Pineapples and even the shoots of young plants are cooked in curries and salads.

Green papayas end up in sumptuous salads, pomelos are perfect complements to minced chicken in glorious blends and mangoes and bananas all are fair game in the cook's savoury domain. Thailand boasts an astonishing 27 varieties of banana, ranging from giant plantains to fragrant dwarf types. Fresh fruits serve best as after meal mouth-fresheners. Apart from the common ones mentioned, there are mangosteens, jackfruit, lychees, hairy rambutan, small light brown fruit called *langsat*, and the durian with its formidable size and thorny skin that has evoked many a rich dissertation.

It is often described (rather unfairly it seems) as "smelling like a cross between rotten garlic and a public convenience". This is journalistic license gone mad surely, and for of the millions of Thais and other Asians, the fruit is something to die for with its rich, sweet buttery texture that is indescribable and has no comparison with any other on this earth.

The Thai word for desserts is "*khanom*", believed to have derived from the argot of the hill tribe of Mon peoples who live in the central plains of Thailand. It actually means crystallised sugar.

Festival Flavours

Thais need very little reason for celebration and there are many traditional festivals and rites of passage that have been an integral part of the culture for centuries. Almost all are associated with food and drink.

Going through the calendar, we begin with *Trut Chin* or Chinese New Year that is celebrated for 15 days, from the first day of the lunar calendar. This does not tally with the Gregorian calendar and tends to fall sometime between the end of January and mid-February. Whatever, it is most impressive in the Chinese dominated provinces and it is when a whole range of specially prepared foods, fruits and ceremonial dishes are trotted out. Houses are cleaned from top to bottom, couplets are specially composed on wall hanging scrolls and many dishes of poultry, pork and sweet cakes are offered to the many deities that occupy the celestial domain.

April 13 sees the start of the Thai New Year or *Songkran*, a word that means "move" as it is the day when the sun changes its position in the celestial firmament. It is when people from rural areas working in cities return home to celebrate *en famille*. It is also known as the "Water Festival" as people believe that water will wash away bad luck, a reverent tradition for the entire Thai community. It is a time when family members gather under one roof to express their respect to elders by pouring rose and jasmine-scented water onto their hands. Presents are also given to make merit and in homage to ancestors.

The elders in return wish the youngsters good luck and prosperity. After performing a bathing rite for Buddha, celebrants both young and old, joyfully splash water on each other. In Thai temples throughout the world, this ritual is practised with much mirth and plenty of drenching.

In May, Chiang Mai bursts into colour and noise during the Intakin festival celebrated at Wat Chedi Luang and all over the city. It is a festival in homage to the city's guardian deity and also in reverent hope that prayers sent forth will ensure the expected monsoon rains to come in time to produce another bountiful harvest. And as always, food is of paramount importance as part of this ritual. Many special dishes are prepared the like of which are rarely seen in restaurants.

There will be copious amounts of glutinous rice, all placed on banana leaf folded and sculpted like verdant works of living art. Whole pig heads, chicken, duck and pork dishes accompany a range of fresh tropical fruits and condiments. At around the same time, when mangoes are at their most luscious, village folk celebrate with all seriousness, a mango fair. Homage to food is as important as that to deities in the Thai culture. Indeed, few if any festivals do not embrace one food or another.

One of the most interesting festivals in Thailand celebrates vegetarianism. This is the annual *Thetsakaan Kin Jay* that begins on the first day of the 9th lunar month and lasts for nine days. Basically, it is a Chinese festival of Taoist Lent where devout Buddhists eschew the eating of meat so they can cleanse their bodies, wherein sit their souls, in homage to the Taoist pantheon of the Nine Emperor Gods known as *Kow Wong Ya* in Cantonese.

On the 15th day of the tenth lunar month, usually around September, Thailand celebrates *Sart*. It refers to merit-making activities at a time food crops begin to ripen and a wide assortment is mature enough to be eaten. The belief is that by appeasing the deities, starvation will be held at bay. *Krayasart*, which means "food for the *sart* rite" is prepared from rice, mung beans, sesame and sugar cooked into a sticky paste, then wrapped with a banana leaf. These are offered to monks, often placed directly into alms bowls arranged on a raised-platform in the temple grounds and transferred into bamboo baskets by the temple attendants. After finishing their main meal, monks would then eat *krayasart* as their dessert.

Tak Bat Devo and *Chak Phra* festivals celebrate the return of the Lord Buddha's return to earth at the end of the rainy season, usually in October. It is a Buddhist belief that during the beginning of Rains Retreat or 'Khao Phansa' Lord Buddha goes to heaven to deliver a sermon to his mother who died after giving birth to him (then Prince Siddharatha) and is born again in heaven. Upon completing his mission in heaven, Lord Buddha then returns to earth and is greeted by a crowd of his disciples and followers.

Tak Bat Devo means "offering of food to Buddhist monks" and *Chak Phra* literally means "pulling of the Buddhist monks" and these festivals are celebrated in many southern provinces such as Nakhon Si Thammarat, Pattani, Phatthalung, Songkhla, and Yala. The most impressive *Chak Phra* festival is on the Tapir River in Surat Thani Province. To mark this occasion, two float-pulling ceremonies are held, one on land and the other on water. On land, beautifully decorated floats are pulled across the town by the participants of the ceremony.

At the same time, on water, the ceremony is highlighted by a float decorated in brilliant colours which is then towed to the middle of the river for a religious ceremony. On the following day, the float carrying the Buddha image is towed along the river so that so that people can worship and make merit. In *Tak Bat Devo*, a row of Buddhist monks, headed by the image of a standing Buddha carried by men representing God Indra and God Brahma, move slowly along a path arranged in advance. People then offer a variety of food and fruit to the passing monks.

The festival of the Illuminated Boat Procession or "Lai Reua Fai" is held at the end of October to celebrate the end of the Buddhist Rains Retreat or "Ork Phansa". It is an ancient tradition of the Northeastern people. In the past, the festival was held in several provinces in this region, but today only some provinces still preserve this tradition, especially *Nakhon Phanom* where the annual event draws thousands of visitors. Originally, the boats were made of banana logs or bamboo but modern versions can be made of wood or synthetic materials. Inside the boats are placed sweets, steamed glutinous rice wrapped in banana leaves and other offerings. Just before sunset, the illuminated boats are prepared for launching on the Mekong River in a spectacular display. Buddhist monks will be invited to chant and deliver a sermon. Participants must bring joss sticks and candles to take part in a religious rite.

Loy Krathong is one of the most popular festivals of Thailand celebrated annually on the full-moon day of the 12th lunar month sometime in mid-November. It takes place at a time when the weather is fine as the rainy season is over and there is a high water level all over the country. "Loy" means "to float" and a "krathong" is a lotus-shaped vessel made of banana leaves. The *krathong* usually contains a candle, three joss sticks, some flowers and coins. The festival is of Hindu Brahmin origin in which people offer thanks to the Goddess of the water. By moonlight, people light the candles and joss sticks, make a wish and launch their *krathongs* on canals, rivers or even small ponds. It is believed that the *krathongs* will carry away sins and bad luck.

Yi Peng is the northern version of *Loy Krathong*, when the cool winds blow through the forests and fields of rice are heavy with ripened grain. In the northern dialect "Yi" means two and "Peng" means "full moon" and the festival is celebrated in the glow of the full moon in the 12th lunar month. Locals accord it another reverent reason; that of showing penitence to the River Goddess, the river being their very life, providing sustenance and a living. Beauty contests are an essential part of the festival and the prettiest Chiang Mai women parade their comely charms on elaborately decorated floats.

Remarkable Renaissance

Where once Western chefs were chary of trying their hands at making Thai spice blends, they are now as enthusiastic about preparing green curries, as they are about Coq au Vin. As supply met demand, many ingredients that were once unavailable except in specialist stores are now featured in mainstream multiple high street shops.

Such a phenomemon can only add to the remarkable renaissance of a splendid cuisine when, for example, European heritage is infused into Thai cuisine. Like language, cuisine is dynamic and enriched with elements of a different genre to suit contemporary needs. Intelligently done, little of the traditional essence need be lost. I have eaten of the most sumptuous of meals prepared by European chefs who marry foie gras with tamarind, lemon grass with salmon and many other "fusion" hybrids that in no way detracts from the classicism of Thai dishes, even if purists may carp. The following pages feature the guest chefs and contributors to this book, some of whom are not of Thai heritage, but nevertheless have earned their onions in their creative interpretation of the cuisine.

Chef Profiles

UK

Mrs Somkid Bhanubandh

This bubbly and ebullient dynamo has the distinction of not only being a first class chef, but also the wife of a Thai prince, the grandson of one of the Thai Chakri kings. Being married into the royal family, she has had first-hand opportunity to learn all about royal Thai cuisine, a distinctive school in its own right within the spectrum of Thai cooking. Somkid has been running her Thai restaurants in Eastbourne since the 1990s and has firmly established Thai cuisine in this coastal resort town. She first established Seeracha in Eastbourne some 13 years ago and opened the Thai Marina in 1999 where it has been drawing in the crowds from day one. This waterfront area is Eastbourne's most prestigious residential area, and having had tutelage from past masters in royal Thai banquets that legions of glitterati, visiting royalty and heads of state have had the privilege to taste, she has naturally introduced many stars of this cuisine into her menu.

Mrs Tym Srisawatt

Former owner of Mantanah in South Norwood, Tym is also the driving force in the Thai Restaurant Association's efforts to upgrade and authenticate the cuisine. Under her steering hand in the kitchen, Mantanah won many awards especially for vegetarian and Northern Thai dishes. Now entrenched in Eastbourne as consultant to Marina Thai and Seeracha, Tym puts her particular stamp in the menus of these two establishments. Married to a Malaysian, Tym has the added advantage of being exposed to another cuisine that is closely related to hers, enriching her understanding of the culinary evolution of the region.

Khun Sunant Wiliarat (Madam Pa)

A bonny and amply proportioned lady whose real name is Khun Sunant Wiliarat, she grew up in the extended royal Thai court where her mother was a cook in the royal kitchens. Learning at her mother's knee, she never intended to become a professional chef. However, she soon found herself working as head chef leading a crew of nine in a large restaurant. Her famous green curry went on to win her many accolades and in 1984, Madam Pa moved to Chao Khun, a Thai restaurant that had more than 1,000 covers. It was a matter of time before she was poached by the Blue Elephant group to man the kitchens of their expanding group in Brussels, London and Paris. Such is Madam Pa's reputation that whenever Her Majesty The Queen of Thailand visits Europe, she will be summoned to prepare her favourite curries in the royal suites of which capital the Queen happens to be staying. As an undisputed queen herself, albeit of curries, Madam Pa still does not speak English.

Vatcharin Bhumichitr

A graduate of the College of Fine Art, Bangkok, Vatcharin Bhumichitr moved to London in 1976 to continue his studies at the London College of Printing. In 1981, he opened a shop in central London specialising in craftwork from Thailand. The Thai Shop was also the first to import authentic ingredients for Thai cooking, a move which helped launch the incredible boom in Thai restaurants that has transformed the British food scene over the past 20 years. Over the years, he has opened five restaurants: The Chiang Mai in London's Soho, The Thai Garden in the East End, The Thai Bistro in Chiswick, The Chiang Rai in Manchester and his current restaurant Southeast W9 in Maida Vale which serves the food of Thailand, Laos, Kampuchea, Vietnam, Myanmar, Malaysia and Singapore. Vatch is perhaps best known as the author of a series of major books on Thai cuisine and culture starting with *The Taste of Thailand* (1988), *Thai Vegetarian Cooking* (1991), *Vatch's Thai Cookbook* (1994), *Vatch's Southeast Asian Cookbook* (1997) and *Vatch's Southeast Asian Salads* (2001).

Australia
Neil Perry

One of Australia's leading and most influential chefs, and now a global culinary figure with a finely-honed knowledge for Asian cuisines, Neil is best known for his award-winning Rockpool restaurant in Sydney, two books, *Rockpool* and *Simply Asian*, four classical recipe CDs and his own range of food products with a definite Asian slant. His most recent eatery is simply called XO, located at Potts Point. The Sydney Morning heralds sums him succinctly: "Neil Perry whose passion, skill and leadership make him an ambassador for modern Australian cooking and throughout the world." Yet, he began his career in the humblest fashion, as a restaurant manager in McMahons Point and then at Rose Bay. By the time he was 24, he had discovered his calling and over the years, learnt his onions from such august names as Damien Pignolet, Stephanie Alexander and David Thompson. Six years after opening Rockpool, it was voted Sydney's Best New Restaurant, the first of many he was to garner over the years. Neil Perry's passion for freshness and quality of Australian produce and Australian style has been forefront in creating a distinguishable style to the rest of the world. He has prepared food for Hollywood celebrity Whoopi Goldberg at the Oscar Awards for the Cherry Blossom Festival in Japan, for Collette Dinnigan at the Paris fashion awards and for the ACO in Hampshire, to name but a few overseas highlights.

David Thompson

David first found fame with the establishment of his first Thai restaurant, Darley Street Thai in Sydney. For 15 years, he has researched Thai culinary techniques and recipes in a way that has evolved and delivered a new paradigm in Thai food in the West. David Thompson's remarkable influence on Thai cooking is most clearly in evidence when he was approached by the Thai government for culinary consultation purposes at the famous Thai cooking institute, Suan Dusit in Bangkok. Subsequently, he has been assisting in the development of their entire curriculum as well as recording and annotating old recipes before they are irretrievably lost. He is today recognised by the Thai Government as one of the world's leading experts on Royal Thai Cuisine, manifest in the menu of Nahm in London's Halkin Hotel. In 2001, David opened Nahm at the Halkin Hotel in Belgravia. Since its launch, Nahm has received constant critical acclaim, resulting in the restaurant becoming the first Thai restaurant ever to be awarded a Michelin Star.

USA

Ken Hom

Born in Tucson, Arizona and raised in Chicago, Illinois, Ken read History of Art at the University of California and also studied at the University of Aix-en-Provence. He learnt to cook from the age of 11, when he started working in his uncle's Chinese restaurant in Chicago after school and at weekends. In order to help pay his university fees, he gave cooking lessons that proved so popular, he was recommended to the Culinary Academy. Ken has taught many great chefs such as Charlie Trotter from Chicago, and when the BBC was looking for a Chinese chef to produce a new series, he was recommended by Madhur Jaffrey who had seen him giving lessons in California. This was the start of his UK TV career with his first series Ken Hom's Chinese Cookery in 1984. He went on to front many others and is now acclaimed as the world's leading authority on Chinese cookery and has cooked for many heads of state. At various times in his professional life, he has been consultant to such august companies as Cathay Pacific Airlines, The Peninsula, Hong Kong, The Oriental, Bangkok, The QE2, Chewton Glen, Hampshire, England and several Yellow River Cafés.

Philippa Kingsley

Her passion for things Thai goes back a long way, from the time she was working as a promotions executive for *Vogue* magazine. Abandoning this glamorous career, Philippa enrolled in Ken Lo's Cookery School at which this book's author was teaching Asian cooking. Ten years on, she has taken on the spiritual name "Khun Pimpa" after immersing herself completely in Thai culture, taken courses in the famous Oriental Cookery School in Bangkok and even a stint in the kitchens of the Blue Elephant Restaurant. Today, Philippa holds court as a Thai cuisine expert in Atlanta, running classes, catering to banquets and writing articles on Buddhism, Thai food and the complete charms of the Thai for the Thai Association magazine. A member of the American Institute of Wine and Food, she also owns and runs Philippa's Orient Inc. She is the only non-Thai person to serve on the Board of The Thai Association of Georgia, and recently catered at a Thai night for the daughter of the cousin of the Thai King. Philippa has had the honour of being received by her Majesty, Queen Sirikit.

Rujireka Souwapawong (Reka)

Reka was born in the southernmost province of Yala, Thailand. She opened her first restaurant in New York's Westchester County in 1985, followed by her second Thai restaurant, Reka's in White Plains in 1987. An Honorary Chairperson of Small Business Advisory Council of New York, she was awarded the "New York 2003 Business Man of the Year". She has appeared in cooking shows on the TV Food Network, organised cooking demonstrations for schools and colleges, including the Culinary Institute of America and the James Beard Foundation. She grew up among an extended family and learnt how to cook, carve vegetables, fold banana leaves and all the tricks of the Thai kitchen from her mother, who became a committed vegetarian. Later in life, she learnt many vegetarian dishes.

Singapore

Sam Leong

Recognised as one of the youngest chefs in Asia, and director of kitchens in Singapore's largest Asian restaurant group, Sam is the maestro behind Paddy Fields regularly listed as among the most authentic Thai restaurants in Singapore. His first experience with the culinary arts began with working for his father—the "King of Shark's Fin"—a respected chef in his own right who ran their highly popular family restaurant in Malaysia. Testament to his hard work and skill, Sam has won numerous accolades, including the prestigious World Gourmet Summit Award of Excellence for Best Asian Ethnic Chef in 2001 and 2002. He has had the honour of participating at the Wolfgang-Lazaroff American Wine & Food Festival as a guest chef. 2001 marked Sam's fourth year cooking at the "Meals on Wheels" charity event in Los Angeles. He has had the honour of cooking for former US president Bill Clinton and Singapore's Senior Minister Goh Chok Tong.

Bangkok
Blue Elephant Cookery School

Rungsan Mulijan (Chang) was born and raised in Bangkok and first worked in the Wangkeo Thai restaurant in 1983. Two years later, he moved to Brussels to work in the Blue Elephant. From here on he worked his way up first in London, then Paris and eventually Corporate Chef for the group. Actively involved in the group's expansion plans, Chang has spearheaded the establishment's new restaurants in Dubai, New Delhi, Beirut, Lyon and Malta. His skills have been so much in demand that he has given demonstrations around the world, notably at the Olympia Food Show in London and on television. He was the prime mover in setting up the Blue Elephant Cooking School and Restaurant in Bangkok in 2002. This culinary landmark, located within a stunning century-old Thai mansion in the heart of the Surasak area incorporates the school and restaurant. The ambience is a regal sweep of traditional Thai architecture and eclectic touches of old-world charm with high ceilings, picture windows and exotic palms. Cookery students come from all over the world and the restaurant headed by Chang acts as a magnet for Bangkok's well-heeled businessmen and ladies.

Chiang Mai Cookery School

Proprietor Sompan Nabnian always had an avid interest in cooking and when he married his English girlfriend, Elizabeth, they decided to start a cookery school. Their first move was to make for England where he decided it was important to cut his culinary teeth by cooking Thai food for westerners, and also having in mind what indigenous ingredients he could adapt to Thai recipes. They returned to his hometown of Chiang Mai in 1993 and started their school in earnest–the first in this northern region. The school has grown both in stature and scope and today many students come from overseas. It was a matter of time before the Nabnians decided a restaurant was in order and they opened The Wok so that their cooking could be accessible to a wider market. The school has a lovely setting, adjoining their home and the teaching area is spread over a handsome tiled court with individual hands-on stations around the perimeter. A long rectory table serves as a dining area for students and guests and all around is an herby Garden of Eden with lemon grass, lime leaves, screwpine (*toei*) bushes, Thai fruits and every conceivable fresh ingredient you would want.

Thai Cooking Utensils and Terms

The traditional Thai kitchen is a simple one, and in earlier times, it was almost always apart from the main house. Central to this is a stove, usually made of clay or terracotta–still much in use in rural areas. But of all the other functional pieces of equipment, the mortar and pestle–usually made of granite–is of prime importance. Of course in today's mores and with urban people living in high rises, modern utensils and food processors play an equally integral role.

A Thai kitchen does not feature a whole host of implements and tools. What constitutes an adequate kitchen would be a wok, a few metal or earthenware pots, a steamer either of aluminium or woven bamboo, a granite or terracotta pestle and mortar, various tools for scraping and processing ingredients such as coconuts and root vegetables, various baskets of woven screwpine (*toei*) leaves for storage and service, a cleaver, a sharp paring knife and a chopping block. Of course, in affluent homes today, there would be a range of high tech implements like grinders, processors and such like to make short work of food processing. While they do not impart a rustic tone, they make short work of many laborious chores.

One of the earliest Thai stoves was an earthenware tray with one side raised to hold the bottom of a cooking pot; charcoal or wood embers were placed under the pot. This was called a *cherng kran* and is all but impossible to find these days. Today, more commonly used are built-in ranges made of tiled cement or terracotta.

Claypots have in fact been in use for thousands of years and many evolved from the traditional shape, the *maw din*. This is a fat-bottomed utensil, tapering towards the neck, the better to ensure minimal evaporation when cooking rice. Like most other Asian cooks, Thais use a wok called *krata,* but earlier models were of clay rather than metal.

The Thai kitchen also features an assortment of wicker and bamboo baskets of many different shapes and sizes for storing dry ingredients or even for serving rice. Cutting and shredding tools run the gamut of cleavers, paring knives and one specifically for carving fruits and vegetables. This is a curved blade mounted on a wooden handle and quite small. Heavy bladed ones are used to cleave through bone, large root vegetables and bamboo.

One traditional piece of equipment is the coconut grater, which is used to prise the meat from the nut before it is grated either in a food processor or a traditional hand-cranked rotating spindle that clamps onto a table top. For the most part, Thai chefs would prefer to process their coconut milk from the fresh nut than rely on the canned variety.

As many Thai dishes tend to be called in their national language, translating menus can be a problem as you will have noticed in different Thai cookbooks where the same dish seems to take on different Thai names in the alphabet spelling. In this book, I have attempted to get as near as possible to the phonetics of the language, and the English spellings echoing the tonal sounds of Thai dishes. Thus, crab is "*puu*" and pork is "*muu*" the double "u" indicating a stretched sound rather than a clipped one. There can be no absolute right or wrong, only a consistency to avoid confusion. I hope you will find this a handy instant guide to facilitate translations of types of dishes, whether encountered in a restaurant or cookbook. For instance, anything with the *yam* reference is a salad. Anything with "*gai*" in it means a chicken dish. Anything with "*phad*" means stir-fried and "*thot*" means deep-fried, apropos most Thai dishes are named with the major ingredients in tandem with the method in which they are cooked.

Methods

Boiling–*tom*
Blanching–*luak*
Steaming–*neung*
Double-boiling–*dtun*
Grilling–*ping* or *yang*
Dry roasting (wok)–*krua*
Baking (oven)–*op*
Deep-frying–*thot*
Stir-fried–*phad*

Descriptions

Raw–*deep*
Spicy–*phet*
Sweet–*wan*
Chinese–*tjin*
Bitter–*khom*
Salty–*khem*
Rich–*rot jat*
Bland–*chud*
Sour–*peaw*
Hot (temperature)–*rawn*
Cold (temperature)–*yen*
Salad–*yam*
Curry–*gaeng*
Soup–*gaeng chud*

Utensils

Woven baskets–*kra-tip khao*
Wok–*krata*
Serving bowls–*chaam*
Small stone mortar–*khrok*
Large earthenware mortar–*khrok din*
Pestle–*saak*
Plate–*jaan*
Spoon–*chawn*
Chopsticks–*ta-kiap*
Fork–*sawn*
Stove–*tao fai*
Cup–*thuay*
Cleaver–*bang taw*
Steamer–*lang theung*
Claypot–*maw din*

Ingredients

Chicken–*gai*
Beef–*nuea*
Crab–*puu*
Duck–*phed*
Fish–*pla*
Pork–*muu*
Prawns–*gung*
Squid–*pla meuk*

Rice noodles (thin or thick)–*kway teow*
Egg–*khai*
Vegetables (general)–*phak*
Lemon grass–*takrai*
Ginger–*khing*
Shallots–*horm daeng*
Garlic–*kratiem*
Coriander–*phak chee*

Seafood (general)–*thalay*
Coconut milk–*kati*
Coconut water–*nam maprao*
Sweets–*khanom*
Soy sauce–*nam see yiew*
Fish sauce–*nam pla*
Chilli sauce dip–*nam prik*
Tamarind sauce–*nam makarm*

All Thai dishes have specific names, some relating to the key ingredients and others of a more romantic or historical description. Their English translations in phonetics are often cause for confusion and a minefield of inconsistencies, as one can judge from restaurant menus. For instance, *gaeng* (curry) is often spelt *kaeng* or *geng* all of which in verbal usage sound nearly the same. Chicken is called *gai* or *kai*, the guttural "g" sounding much like a soft "k". The English names here are universally acceptable and the phonetics are as near as we can get to the actual pronunciation.

The Thai Store Cupboard

1   2   3   4, 5

1 Salted soy beans (*tau jiew*) Fermented and salted yellow beans that came by way of China and when crushed, become the commonly used yellow bean sauce. Indispensable in fish dishes and as flavouring for vegetable stir-fries. 2 Pickled capers Capers originate from various parts of the Mediterranean. Pickled capers are made by allowing the capers to wilt for a day under strong sunlight before soaking them in brine. Pickled capers are sour and salty, and should always be kept in their pickling solution if not in use. 3 Prawn (shrimp) paste (*kapi*) Often reviled as "smelling like hell" but integral to almost all spice pastes. They range from pale pink to dark brown and should always be toasted or cooked before being eaten as a dip or in curry pastes. A little goes a long way so use sparingly. It should be stored well wrapped up and away from other foods.

6   7   8, 9   10   11

4 Coriander seeds (*luk pak chi*) Coriander seeds are small, dark brown pips that have a much stronger flavour than the leaves and are usually ground up for curry powders. 5 Cumin (*mellet yira*) The Thai name tends to embrace its two cousins, fennel and caraway. It is a principal curry powder ingredient used for its sweet flavour. 6 Hang Lay curry powder (*phong kari*) Hang Lay is typically a blend of ground cumin, turmeric, coriander and mace powder. There are many variations, such as the version found on page 38. 7 Chilli oil (*prik khao soi*) Typically used as added colour and spice to curries, chilli oil is available in most Chinese and Thai stores. 8 Candlenuts Oily and waxy, candlenuts are similar to the macadamia nut in terms of oil content. Apart from culinary purposes, they have also been employed in traditional medicine for various ailments, such

as constipation. 9 Cardamom (*luk grawan*) Pale green pods containing tiny black seeds with a pungent flavour used mainly in Massaman curry pastes. 10 Dried prawns (shrimp) (*gung haeng*) Indispensable to every Thai kitchen, they are soaked and ground into pastes or added to salads for their rich, smoky flavour. Before using, prawns should be soaked to remove some of the shell dust incurred in the drying process. Indispensable in salad dressings, a handful of dried prawns make a good, almost fish sauce-like seasoning for soups. Dried prawns can also be a milder substitute to stronger-flavoured prawn paste. 11 Whole grain mustard This condiment has a mild sweet flavour, with a grainy texture and is paired with cold cuts of meat or added to sauces and dressings for an extra dimension.

12

13

15 16 17 18 19

12 Turmeric *(kamin)* As a fresh ingredient and a cousin of ginger, it has an indelible yellow/orange colour and pleasant pungency for rice dishes and yellow curries. Dried turmeric is but a pale shadow of the fresh root. 13 Pea aubergines *(makreua puang)* are, as the name suggests, pea-size and hard as nuts. These are rarely eaten raw and taste better cooked. 14 Sweet (Thai) basil *(bai horapa)* An aromatic leaf that is quite different from the European variety and used lavishly in salads, curries and stir-fries, sweet basil is a purple-stalked, green herb with an aniseed and mint flavour. It does not keep well and should be used up within a day or two, or they go limp and turn brown. 15 Apple aubergines or globe aubergines are green, yellow, orange or purple, some with white streaks. When cutting them before

cooking, always soak in cold water with a little lemon juice to prevent discolouration. Very crunchy in texture, they can be eaten raw in salads. 16 Water convolvulus *(pak bung)* An aquatic plant with hollow stems and thin green leaves, water convolvulus is packed with nutrition and flavour. Also known as morning glory, *kang kong* or swamp cabbage in America. 17 Kaffir lime *(makrut)* A gnarled fruit, also called the leprous lime on account of its corrugated skin. Kaffir limes are valued for the zest that its grated skin produces. 18 Water chestnut *(haew)* Small, dark skinned nuts with a crisp texture and elusive sweetness eaten for its cooling properties. Fresh water chestnuts are fiddly to prepare, while canned varieties come ready peeled and still maintain their crunch. 19 Sawtooth coriander *(pak chi*

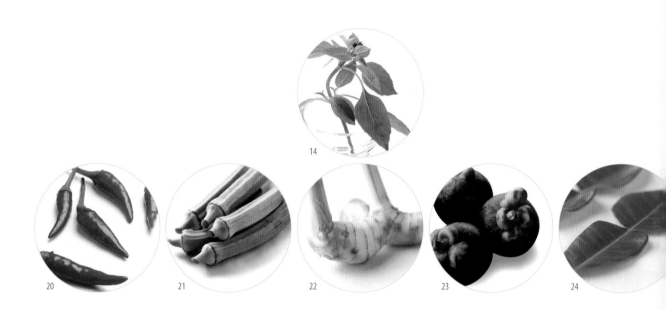

14

20 21 22 23 24

farang) The Thai name for this aromatic herb translates to "foreign coriander" with the tongue-twisting botanical name of "eryngo" of the sawtooth family. Each serrated leaf is about 5-cm (2-in) long, with a delicious fragrance. 20 Bird's eye chillies *(prik ki nu)* The cornerstone of Thai cooking, chillies come in a rainbow range that can be extremely fiery or very mild. The best known are bird's eye chillies, that have earned a somewhat infamous name for the potent fire in Thai cooking. Dried versions are used mainly in curry pastes. *Prik chi fa* is the longer variety and not as potent. It is often sliced and fried as a garnish or cut to resemble flowers for decoration. 21 Ladies fingers *(khajiab mawn)* Also known as okra, this vegetable, with a rather slimy texture when cooked, is indigenous to most of

Asia and particularly in Indian cooking. It can only be eaten cooked, boiled as a salad ingredient or stir-fried with chilli or curry paste. 22 Galangal *(kha)* Ranging from ivory to pale yellow in colour, with pink-tinged tips at its bulbous ends, galangal, like ginger, is a member of the rhizome family. It has a sharp and refreshing flavour, and is an indispensable ingredient in many Thai curries. Also known as Laos root or blue ginger. 23 Mangosteen A thick-fleshed, purple fruit with chalk white sweet and astringent cloves of flesh. A delicious and cooling fruit, it can be eaten fresh or cooked in salads. 24 Kaffir lime leaves Together with lemon grass and galangal, this forms a Thai holy trinity. The leaf has a heady fragrance and perfumes soups and curries to a heavenly degree for which there is no substitute.

Curries, Dips and Pastes

The spectrum of curries is wide and this section includes all types of main ingredients like poultry, meat, seafood and vegetables. This is a classification that lauds Thai curries, as they constitute the mainstay of most meals. Developed over many centuries, most pastes are family recipes handed down the generations and use much the same basic spices and herbs.

With the plethora of dried spices, powders and fresh herbs, the permutations are endless. The fundamental rule of thumb is that preparation of curry pastes is not an exact science and proportions vary depending on personal taste. Some are more robust than others, the amount of chilli fire highly dependent on specific taste; more or less not distracting from the basic flavour.

The aromatics like lemon grass, garlic, galangal, ginger, lime leaves and basil work in perfect tandem with the dried spices. Chopped, ground or puréed, each method is dictated by the nature of a particular curry—smooth, hearty or richly textured.

Thai curries can be classified into three main types—red, green and Massaman style. There is a less common yellow curry called Hang Lay curry, that came by way of her Malaysian neighbour, its characteristic colour derived from the use of fresh or powdered turmeric.

Specifically, Thai curries are called *gaeng phed*, which translates to 'thickened spicy liquids'. At the other end of this spectrum are the *gaeng chud*, which are unspiced and often relegated for use in soups.

There are regional differences; northern Thailand derives much influence from neighbouring Myanmar, which has a strong Indian culinary heritage that uses many dried spices and powders. To the south, curries often feature spices such as cumin, cardamom, fenugreek and turmeric.

What may pass as a humble dip or side sauce in other Asian cuisines is seen in a totally different light within the pantheon of Thai menus. Indeed, many a main course dish would be a pale shadow of itself but for the accompaniment of a spicy dip or two. Whatever the concoction, each is of paramount importance in the ultimate enjoyment of a dish. Chillies and lime, ginger and chopped nuts, coriander and mint—the list is endless and each has a reverent place on the Thai table.

The following recipes for curry pastes make enough for 1 kg (2 lb 3 oz) meat or seafood, bearing in mind individual taste for strength of paste. As a rough guide, 3 Tbsp paste will suffice for 450 g (1 lb) meat or seafood.

Hang Lay Curry Powder Phong Kari

This version comes courtesy of Sompan Nabnian of the Chiang Mai Cookery School. He says to simply blend equal quantities of cumin, turmeric, coriander and mace powder and keep in an airtight jar.

Ground cumin 2 Tbsp

Ground turmeric 2 Tbsp

Ground coriander 2 Tbsp

Ground mace 2 Tbsp

1 Combine ingredients and mix well. Store in an airtight container away from direct sunlight until use.

Yellow Curry Paste Nam Prik Gaeng Liang

Ground coriander 2 Tbsp

Ground cumin 1 tsp

Lemon grass 2 stalks, tough outer leaves removed and finely chopped

Dried chillies 6, to soften

Prawn (shrimp) paste 1 Tbsp

Turmeric 2.5-cm (1-in) knob, peeled and finely chopped

Onion 1, large, peeled and sliced

Garlic 4 cloves, peeled and finely chopped

Galangal 2.5-cm (1-in) knob, peeled and finely chopped

Cooking oil 180 ml (6 fl oz / $^3/_4$ cup)

Salt 1 tsp

1 Heat a frying pan over low heat. Dry-fry coriander and cumin for 8 minutes, or until fragrant. Remove from heat and set aside.

2 Using a mortar and pestle, pound lemon grass and chillies until fine.

3 Transfer mixture to a blender. Add prawn paste, turmeric, onion, garlic and galangal. Blend into a fine paste. Add cumin, coriander and salt. Mix well.

4 Heat oil over medium heat. Fry paste for 10 minutes, or until oil begins to exude from mixture.

5 Remove from heat and set aside to cool. Store in an airtight container and refrigerate until use.

Red Curry Paste Nam Prik Gaeng Daeng

Ground coriander 2 Tbsp

Ground cumin 1 Tbsp

Lemon grass 2 stalks, tough outer leaves removed and finely chopped

Black peppercorns 1 tsp

Dried chillies 10, soaked to soften

Prawn (shrimp) paste 1 Tbsp

Onion 1, large, peeled and finely chopped

Garlic 4 cloves, peeled and finely chopped

Galangal 2.5-cm (1-in) knob, peeled and finely chopped

Kaffir lime leaves 4

Salt 1 tsp

Cooking oil 180 ml (6 fl oz / $^3/_4$ cup)

1 Heat a frying pan over medium heat. Dry-fry coriander and cumin for 8 minutes, or until fragrant. Remove from heat and set aside.

2 Using a mortar and pestle, pound lemon grass, peppercorns and chillies until fine.

3 Transfer mixture to a blender. Add prawn paste, onion, garlic, galangal and kaffir lime leaves and blend into a fine paste. Add cumin, coriander and salt. Mix well.

4 Heat oil over medium heat. Fry paste for 10 minutes, or until oil begins to exude from mixture.

5 Remove from heat and set aside to cool. Store in an airtight container and refrigerate until use.

Red Curry Paste

Massaman Curry Paste

Green Curry Paste

Hang Lay Curry Paste

Massaman Curry Paste
Nam Prik Massaman

Ground coriander 2 Tbsp

Ground cumin 1 Tbsp

Ground turmeric 1 tsp

Chilli powder 1 Tbsp

Lemon grass 2 stalks, tough outer leaves removed and finely chopped

Cardamom pods 2

Galangal 1.5-cm ($^3/_4$-in) knob, peeled and finely sliced

Onion 1, peeled and finely sliced

Garlic 4 cloves, peeled and finely chopped

Prawn (shrimp) paste 1 Tbsp

Cooking oil 180 ml (6 fl oz / $^3/_4$ cup)

1 Heat a frying pan over medium heat. Dry-fry coriander, cumin, turmeric and chilli powder for 8 minutes, or until fragrant. Remove from heat and set aside.

2 Using a mortar and pestle, pound lemon grass, cardamom and galangal until fine.

3 Transfer mixture to a blender (food processor). Add onion, garlic and prawn paste and blend into a fine paste. Add ground spices. Mix well.

4 Heat oil over medium heat. Fry paste for 10 minutes, or until oil begins to exude from mixture.

5 Remove from heat and set aside to cool. Store in an airtight container and refrigerate until use.

Green Curry Paste Nam Prik Gaeng Khiaw Wan

Green chillies 4, seeded and finely chopped

Coriander (cilantro) leaves and root 3 sprigs,
bruised and coarsely chopped

Galangal 2.5-cm (1-in) knob, peeled and
finely sliced

Lemon grass 2 stalks, tough outer leaves
removed and finely chopped

Black peppercorns 1 tsp

Prawn (shrimp) paste 1 Tbsp

Kaffir lime leaves 3

Onion 1, peeled and finely sliced

Garlic 4 cloves, peeled and chopped

Cooking oil 180 ml (6 fl oz / ³/₄ cup)

1 Using a mortar and pestle, pound chillies, coriander, galangal, lemon grass
and peppercorns until fine.

2 Transfer mixture to a blender. Add prawn paste, kaffir lime leaves, onion
and garlic and blend into a fine paste.

3 Heat oil over medium heat and fry paste for 10 minutes, or until oil begins
to exude from mixture.

4 Remove from heat and set aside to cool. Store in an airtight container and
refrigerate until use.

Hang Lay Curry Paste Nam Prik Hang Lay

*This is just one of the many Hang Lay curry pastes kindly given to me by a
Chiang Mai friend who, of course, swears it is the best. It uses three different
types of ginger that characterises its flavour. Other versions use a blend of dry
powders but this is a blend I have used many times. It is as well to make a large
batch as it keeps indefinitely in the fridge.*

Lemon grass 2 stalks, tough outer leaves
removed and cut into 5-cm (2-in)
lengths

Dried chillies 12, soaked to soften

Shallots 8, peeled and chopped

Galangal 1.5-cm (³/₄-in) knob, peeled
and finely sliced

Ginger 2.5-cm (1-in) knob, peeled
and finely chopped

Garlic 12 cloves, peeled and chopped

Turmeric 2.5-cm (1-in) knob, peeled
and finely chopped

Prawn (shrimp) paste 1 Tbsp

Cooking oil 180 ml (6 fl oz / ³/₄ cup)

Fish sauce 1 Tbsp

1 Using a mortar and pestle, pound lemon grass, chillies, shallots and
galangal until fine.

2 Transfer mixture to a blender and add ginger, garlic, turmeric and prawn
paste. Blend into a fine paste.

3 Heat oil over medium heat and fry paste for 10 minutes, or until fragrant
and oil begins to exude from mixture. Add fish sauce and stir well.

4 Remove from heat and set aside to cool. Store in an airtight container and
refrigerate until use.

Northern Chilli Paste

Northern Chilli Paste Nam Prik Pao

Often referred to as Chilli Jam, it is in reality a rich, hot chilli paste that is ubiquitous in Thailand. Practically every chef worth his salt would make his own, but the commercial variety is also available in specialist Thai or Southeast Asian stores. A similar Malaysian version is called sambal grago (dried prawn relish). The traditional and much older method is to grill all the ingredients, but frying is a much easier option.

Cooking oil for deep-frying

Shallots 450 g (1 lb), peeled and sliced

Garlic 200 g (7 oz), peeled and sliced

Dried prawns (shrimps) 60 g (2 oz)

Dried red chillies 12, soaked to soften

Galangal 2.5-cm (1-in) knob, peeled and finely sliced

Prawn (shrimp) paste 2 tsp, dry-fried for 2–3 minutes or until fragrant

Palm sugar 200 g (7 oz)

Fish sauce 2 Tbsp

Tamarind juice 1 Tbsp paste, mixed with 3 Tbsp water and strained

1 Heat oil in a wok over medium heat. In separate batches, deep-fry shallots, garlic, dried prawns and chillies until golden brown and crisp. Drain and reserve 5 Tbsp oil.

2 Combine shallots, garlic, dried shrimps and chillies with galangal and prawn paste in a blender and blend into a fine paste.

3 Heat reserved oil in a pan over medium heat. Transfer paste to pan and stir-fry until fragrant. Add palm sugar, fish sauce and tamarind juice. Stir until paste is thickened and fragrant.

4 Remove from heat and set aside to cool. Store in an airtight container and refrigerate until use.

Dried Prawns, Chillies, Lime and Basil Dip

Young Chilli Dipping Sauce

Dried Prawns, Chillies, Lime and Basil Dip Nam Prik Horapa

A universal condiment for dipping or as a paste for fried vegetables.

Dried prawns (shrimps) 3 Tbsp, soaked to soften and drained
Red chillies 4, finely chopped
Lime juice 60 ml (2 fl oz / ¹/₄ cup)
Sugar 2 tsp
Fish sauce 1 tsp
Sweet basil a few leaves, finely chopped
Water 2 Tbsp

1 Using a mortar and pestle, pound dried prawns and chillies until fine.

2 Transfer to a blender. Add lime juice, sugar, fish sauce, water and basil leaves and blend into a fine paste.

Young Chilli Dipping Sauce Nam Prik Num

Another creation by Sompan Nabnian, this is a typical Northern Thai dipping sauce.

Green chillies 15, large
Garlic 1 bulb
Shallots 9

Prawn (shrimp) paste ¹/₂ tsp
Salt ¹/₂ tsp
Fish sauce 1 Tbsp

1 Preheat oven to 180°C (350°F).

2 Place chillies, garlic and shallots on a baking tray and roast in oven for 10–15 minutes. Seal chillies, garlic and shallots in individual plastic or polythene bags and leave to cool. Peel and discard skin.

3 Using a mortar and pestle, pound chillies, garlic and shallots into a fine paste. Transfer to a mixing bowl and add prawn paste, salt and fish sauce. Mix well.

4 Serve with a selection of fresh, steamed or boiled vegetables such as aubergines, cucumber, carrot, cabbage, long beans, pumpkin and bamboo shoots.

43

Sour Paste

Sour Paste Gaeng Som

Typically used as a base for seafood soups, gaeng som provides a sour, spicy kick for the taste buds.

Bird's eye chillies 10
Coriander leaves (cilantro) 2 sprigs
Onion 1, large, peeled and finely chopped
Garlic 4 cloves, peeled and finely chopped
Prawn (shrimp) paste 1 Tbsp
Tamarind juice 1 Tbsp paste, mixed with 3 Tbsp water and strained

1 Using a mortar and pestle, pound chillies and coriander until fine. Transfer to a blender. Add onion, garlic and prawn paste and blend into a fine paste.

2 Transfer paste to a mixing bowl. Add tamarind juice and mix well.

3 Store in an airtight container and refrigerate until use.

Basic Sweet and Sour Sauce Nam Peaw Wan

There are many variations to this Chinese staple and depending on the regional type; it could be a blend of different ingredients, fundamentally of sweet and sour flavours. For instance, sugar and vinegar are the cornerstones of this sauce. So are tomato and lemon juice, underscoring the yin yang principle of contrasting elements to forge universal harmony. Whatever the blend, the ideal consistency is similar to that of pouring cream. A little corn flour may be added, if preferred as a dip than as a cooking sauce.

Plum sauce 5 Tbsp
Rice vinegar 3 Tbsp
Tomato sauce 2 Tbsp
Pineapple juice 4 Tbsp
Water 200 ml (8 fl oz/ ²/₃ cup
Corn flour (cornstarch) 1 Tbsp, mixed with 3 Tbsp water (optional)

1 Combine ingredients and mix well. Bring to a slow boil in a pot over medium heat for 5 minutes. Add corn flour mixture and mix well to thicken, if desired.

Prawn Paste with Lime Leaf Nam Prik Kapi

A zesty dip for fried seafood or mixed with warm, cooked rice as a quick savoury dish. Traditional dip does not contain lime leaves, but the leaves add a delicious tang.

Dried prawn (shrimp) paste 3.5 x–3.5 x 1-cm
  (1.5 x 1.5 x $^1/_2$-in) block
Red chillies 6, finely chopped
Kaffir lime leaves 4
Lime juice 60 ml (2 fl oz / $^1/_4$ cup)
Salt a pinch
Hot water 1 Tbsp

1 Wrap prawn paste in aluminium foil. Heat a pan over medium heat and toast prawn paste for 2–3 minutes, or until slightly charred. Remove from heat and set aside.

2 Using a mortar and pestle, pound chillies and kaffir lime leaves until fine. Add prawn paste and pound until fine, then transfer mixture to a blender and blend into a fine paste.

3 Transfer paste to a mixing bowl and add lime juice, salt and hot water. Mix well.

4 Serve as a dipping sauce for fried seafood, or mixed with cooked white rice.

Vegetables and Salads

We used to have our own jackfruit tree that hung heavy with jackfruits as large as several footballs. My aunt would leave the really large ones to tree-ripen and knock down the small, green young ones with a long bamboo pole. Cooked in a rich coconut milk curry, jackfruit is sublime served with rice and, for good measure, lumps of durian meat. Perhaps an acquired taste, but this is among my most delicious childhood memories. Use only fresh, unripe jackfruit, as the canned variety tends to look greyish and taste mushy. When you cut into the green jackfruit, a very sticky and gooey sap oozes out that tends to stick to your knife. Oil your knife slightly to counter this.

Jackfruit Curry Gaeng Kanun

Serves 4

Unripe jackfruit 1 kg (2 lb 3 oz), peeled and sliced

Vegetable oil 4 tsp

Coconut milk 625 ml (20 fl oz / 2$\frac{1}{2}$ cups)

Prawns (shrimps) 200 g (7 oz), peeled, leaving tails intact

Fish sauce 2 Tbsp

Sugar 2 tsp

Paste

Dried prawns (shrimps) 3 Tbsp, soaked to soften, then drained

Lemon grass 2 stalks, trimmed, use only 5-cm (2-in) from bulbous end

Red chillies 8, seeded and finely chopped

Candlenuts 6

Onion 1, large, peeled and chopped

Prawn (shrimp) paste 1 Tbsp

Turmeric 2.5-cm (1-in) knob, peeled and chopped

1 Bring a pot of salted water to the boil and add jackfruit. Boil until jackfruit is soft. Drain, rinse in cold water and set aside.

2 Prepare paste. Using a mortar and pestle, combine ingredients and pound until fine.

3 Heat oil in a wok over medium heat and fry paste for 6 minutes, or until fragrant. Reduce heat, add coconut milk and jackfruit and simmer for 5 minutes.

4 Add prawns and simmer until cooked. Add fish sauce and sugar. Stir well, simmer for a few more minutes and remove from heat.

5 Dish out and serve immediately with steamed white rice.

Herein is a curious derivative of the universally loved Indonesian Gado Gado. Both salads are similar and it matters little which is the original, dating as they do centuries back. The sauce is practically the same as Thai satay *sauce and the combination of crunchy raw vegetables and nutty sauce is ambrosial. It can be served warm or cold and is a meal in itself. Water convolvulus is ubiquitous in Thailand and also known as* "kang kong". *Use spinach if this is not available.*

Spicy Vegetable Salad Pak Prik

Serves 4

Vegetable oil 3 Tbsp

Firm bean curd 200 g (7 oz)

Water convolvulus (*kang kong*) 200 g (7 oz)

Cabbage 1 small head, washed and sliced into thin strips

Long beans 10

Bean sprouts 200 g (7 oz), tailed

Cucumber 1, peeled and cut into thin slices

Hard-boiled eggs 4, peeled and sliced

Prawn (shrimp) crackers a handful

Ground peanuts 2 Tbsp

Dipping sauce

Dried chillies 10, seeded and soaked

Prawn (shrimp) paste 1 Tbsp

Onion 1, large, peeled and chopped

Garlic 4 cloves, peeled and chopped

Cooking oil 2 Tbsp

Tamarind juice 2 Tbsp paste, mixed with 500 ml (16 fl oz / 2 cups) water and strained

Ground peanuts 4 Tbsp

Sugar 2 tsp

1 Prepare dipping sauce. Place chillies, prawn paste, onion and garlic in a blender and blend into a fine paste. Heat oil in a pan over medium heat. Fry paste until fragrant, then add tamarind juice. Bring mixture to the boil for 2 minutes and remove from heat. Add ground peanuts and mix well. Set aside.

2 Heat oil in a frying pan over medium heat. Fry bean curd until crisp and light brown. Drain and leave to cool. Cut into thin slices and set aside.

3 Meanwhile, bring a large pot of water to the boil. Blanch water convolvulus, cabbage, long beans and bean sprouts for 3 minutes and drain.

4 Arrange blanched vegetables, cucumber, hard-boiled eggs, bean curd pieces, prawn crackers and ground peanuts on a serving plate. Serve with dipping sauce on the side.

The Indian name for aubergines is brinjal. The long, slender green or purple varieties are more indigenous than the fat, glossy aubergines found in the west. They also have a less cotton-woolly texture as compared to their large purple cousin. Coupled with fermented yellow beans (tau jiew), *this is a deliciously savoury, spicy concoction.*

Spicy Aubergine Salad Phad Makreua Tau Jiew

Serves 4

Green aubergines (eggplants / brinjals) 2

Oil 6 Tbsp

Salt 2 tsp

Sugar 1 Tbsp

Tomato purée 1 Tbsp

Tamarind juice 1 Tbsp paste, mixed with 4 Tbsp water and strained

Preserved yellow bean sauce 1 Tbsp

Paste

Dried red chillies 6, soaked and seeded

Onion 1, large, peeled and finely chopped

Garlic 6 cloves, peeled and finely chopped

Prawn (shrimp) paste 1 Tbsp

1 Cut hard tips off aubergines and slice in half lengthwise. Bring a pot of water to the boil. Blanch aubergines for 2 minutes, drain well and set aside on a serving plate.

2 Prepare paste. Place ingredients in a blender and blend into a fine paste. Heat oil in a wok over medium heat. Fry paste for 4 minutes, or until fragrant.

3 Add salt, sugar, tomato purée, tamarind juice and yellow bean sauce. Reduce heat and stir-fry for 5 minutes, or until fragrant.

4 Drizzle sauce over aubergines and serve immediately.

Tip: As an alternative to blanching, grill aubergines for 6 minutes on each side until cooked through, with slightly charred skin.

This has overtones of Indian cookery, the vegetable a favourite of the sub-continent. When you choose ladies fingers (okra), bend the stalk a little. If it does not snap, the ladies finger is young and tender enough. Select the pale green ones without any blemishes. Chuchi refers to the use of lime peel. In this case, the kaffir lime has a very gnarled, knobby texture. Ordinary green or Jamaican limes will do as well.

Spicy Ladies Fingers Chuchi Khajiab

Serves 4

Ladies fingers (okra) 400 g (14 oz)

Cooking oil 2 Tbsp

Shallots 6, peeled and sliced

Red curry paste (page 39) 2 Tbsp

Kaffir lime zest 1 tsp

Prawns (shrimps) 200 g (7 oz), peeled

Coconut milk 250 ml (8 fl oz / 1 cup)

Fish sauce 1 Tbsp

Sugar 1 tsp

1 Trim stem of ladies fingers. Soak in cold water for a few minutes, drain and set aside.

2 Heat oil in a wok over medium heat. Stir-fry shallots for 2 minutes, or until light brown. Add curry paste and kaffir lime zest and stir-fry until fragrant.

3 Add ladies fingers, prawns, coconut milk, fish sauce and sugar. Stir well and bring to the boil for 2 minutes.

4 Dish out and serve immediately.

The winged bean is a curious-looking green vegetable. It is about 10-cm (4-in) long, with four slightly frilled ridges that resemble wings, hence its name. Crunchy, with a nutty flavour, winged beans are often eaten raw, especially the young tender ones, but are also delicious stir-fried. It is the use of Northern chilli paste (Nam Prik Pao) that characterises the dish.

Stir-fried Winged Beans and Prawns Phad Tua Pluu Gung

Serves 4

Winged beans 400 g (14 oz)

Cooking oil 2 Tbsp

Northern chilli paste (page 42) 2 Tbsp

Lime juice 2 Tbsp

Sugar 1 Tbsp

Prawns (shrimps) 100 g (3¹/₂ oz), cooked and peeled

Coconut milk 2 Tbsp

1   Prepare winged beans. Trim small feathery roots on both ends. Diagonally cut into 1.5-cm (¹/₂-in) lengths. Wash and drain thoroughly.

2   Heat oil in a wok over medium heat. Fry chilli paste until fragrant. Add lime juice and sugar. Stir-fry for 2 minutes, then add winged beans, prawns and coconut milk. Stir constantly, until mixture is thickened.

3   Dish out and serve with steamed white rice.

TYM SRISAWATT

This is one vegetable dish that even serious carnivores would not turn their noses down at. Thai vegetable dishes within the stir-fry realm differ considerably from the Chinese genre, seasonings usually running the gamut of spices or spice paste and often enriched with coconut milk. It is also the kind of dish that allows total ingenuity in the choice of vegetables.

Vegetable Curry Gaeng Nopakkao

Serves 4

Vegetable oil 2 Tbsp

Yellow curry paste (page 38) 2 Tbsp

Coconut milk 180 ml (6 fl oz / ³/₄ cup)

Cabbage 1 small head, cut into quarters

Carrot 1, peeled and finely sliced into strips

Apple aubergines (eggplants / brinjals) 4, large,
    cut into halves

Water convolvulus (*kang kong*) 100 g (3¹/₂ oz)

Fish sauce 1 Tbsp

Palm sugar 1 Tbsp

Coconut cream 3 Tbsp

1　Heat oil in a wok over medium heat. Fry curry paste until fragrant. Add coconut milk and bring mixture to the boil.

2　Add vegetables, fish sauce and palm sugar. Reduce heat and simmer for 8 minutes, or until vegetables are tender.

3　Dish out and drizzle coconut cream over curry. Serve immediately.

Probably one of the most versatile of root vegetables, the large white radish known variously as daikon or mooli can be stir-fried, steamed, boiled, shredded and cooked in a dozen different ways. It has a sweetish flavour not unlike carrot and is marvellous for making this traditional snack. This recipe lists two ways in which the radish cake may be presented.

Steamed Radish Cake Khanom Chai Tau

Makes one 200 g (7 oz) cake

White radishes (*daikon*) 900 g (2 lb), peeled and grated

Rice flour 400 g (14¹/₃ oz)

**Tapioca flour or
corn flour (cornstarch)** 55 g (2 oz)

Water 125 ml (4 fl oz / ¹/₂ cup)

Salt 2 tsp

Cooking oil 2 Tbsp

Vegetable stock cube 1, crushed

1 Place grated radish in a blender and blend until fine. Set aside.

2 Combine both types of flour and sift into a mixing bowl. Gradually add water and mix well. Mixture should be thick and moist. Add salt, oil, stock cube and radish. Mix until well blended.

3 Transfer mixture to a non-stick, medium-sized pot. Cook over low heat for 10 minutes, or until cake is firm. Remove from pot and steam over high heat for 30 minutes. Radish cake is ready when an inserted toothpick comes out clean. Set aside to cool before use.

Pan-fried Radish Cake

Serves 4

Steamed radish cake 200 g (7 oz)

Cooking oil 2 Tbsp

1 Slice radish cake into 5-cm (2-in) squares.

2 Heat oil in a frying pan over medium heat. Fry radish cake pieces until light brown. Drain and serve hot with chilli sauce on the side.

Stir-fried Radish Cake

Serves 4

Steamed radish cake 200 g (7 oz)

Oil 2 Tbsp

Eggs 2, lightly beaten

Prawns (shrimps) 55 g (2 oz), peeled and deveined

Sweet soy sauce 2 Tbsp

Chilli sauce to taste

Spring onion (scallion) 1, finely chopped

1 Slice radish cake into 2.5-cm (1-in) pieces. Heat oil in a frying pan over medium heat. Stir-fry radish cake pieces, eggs and prawns for 3 minutes, or until prawns change colour and are cooked. Add sweet soy sauce and chilli sauce, stir well and remove from heat.

2 Garnish with chopped spring onions. Serve immediately.

*Not quite vegetarian but acceptable to those part-herbivores who do not eschew the occasional fish dish, this is a delicious blend of Thai-Chinese flavours, served in its own pot. Choose a claypot (*maw din*) with glazed interior and a tight lid. Claypots are available from most Chinese supermarkets.*

Fish and Bean Curd in Claypot Pla Orb Tau Hu Maw Din

Serves 4

Snapper fillets 450 g (16 oz 1 lb), cleaned and deboned

Oil for deep-frying

Firm bean curd 200 g (7 oz), cut into 2.5-cm (1-in) cubes

Vegetable oil 2 Tbsp

Ginger 3.5-cm (1¹/₂-in) knob, peeled and finely chopped

Garlic 2 cloves, peeled and finely chopped

Spring onions (scallions) 3, cut into 5-cm (2-in) lengths

Oyster sauce 2 Tbsp

Sesame oil 2 Tbsp

Dark soy sauce 2 Tbsp

Ground black pepper 1 Tbsp

Water 250 ml (10 fl oz / 1 cup)

Corn flour (cornstarch) 1 Tbsp, mixed with 3 Tbsp water

Celery leaves 2 Tbsp, chopped

1 Cut snapper into 4-cm (1¹/₂-in) slices. Set aside.

2 Heat oil for deep-frying over high heat. Deep-fry bean curd until light brown in colour. Remove, drain and set aside.

3 Using a clean pan, heat vegetable oil over medium heat. Stir-fry ginger and garlic for 1 minute. Add spring onions, oyster sauce, sesame oil, soy sauce and pepper. Stir-fry for 1 minute, then add snapper, deep-fried bean curd and corn flour mixture. Stir well and cook for 5–7 minutes, or until sauce is thickened and snapper is cooked.

4 Meanwhile, heat a claypot over medium heat for 5 minutes. Transfer snapper and bean curd to claypot. Serve immediately, garnished with celery leaves.

RUJIREKA SOUWAPAWONG

Growing up in an idyllic setting in South Thailand and learning all crafts of the Thai kitchen, Reka remembers cooking water convolvulus, also known as morning glory, kang kong *or Thai spinach, with their characteristic hollow stems and small, delicately flavoured leaves. Water convolvulus is indigenous to most of tropical Asia and thrives well in marshy soil, even in ponds and river estuaries. Before cooking, it is best to split their hollow stems as creepy crawlies often burrow in them to nest. Some restaurants in Thailand are famous for their variations of the dish. Others make a showpiece of it by tossing the vegetables so high it is called Pad Bung Loi Fa meaning "flying sky high morning glory".*

Stir-fried Water Convolvulus Pak Pug Bung Fai Dang

Serves 4

Vegetable oil 1 Tbsp

Chopped garlic 1 Tbsp

Water convolvulus (*kang kong*) 450 g (1 lb), cut into 5-cm (2-in) lengths, washed and drained

Red capsicum (bell pepper) 1, cored, seeded and finely sliced

Fish sauce 1 Tbsp

Oyster sauce 1 Tbsp

1 Heat oil in a wok or frying pan over medium heat. Stir-fry garlic for 1 minute. Increase heat and add water convolvulus and capsicum and stir-fry quickly for 1–2 minutes. Moisture should exude from the water convolvulus.

2 Add fish sauce and oyster sauce. Stir-fry for 1 minute before removing from heat. Serve immediately.

Tip: For a more substantial dish, add a handful of raw, peeled prawns or any other meat and stir-fry until cooked, before adding the water convolvulus leaves.

SAM LEONG

There's a fragrant ring to this dish that could cross over to the dessert sector, but is a unique vegetarian creation in its own right. As Director of Kitchens for Tung Lok Group of restaurants, Sam really cuts his teeth on a wide spectrum of Asian cuisines, and is not above the odd fusion thing or two.

Lychees have no peer for taste, fragrance and sweetness and the dressing is a cornucopian offering of peppery, sharp and aromatic flavours. This is handsome enough to pass off as a main entrée.

Lychee, Lychee, Lychee Fields Forever Yam Linchi

Serves 4

Fresh lychees 24, peeled and seeded or use canned lychees

White button mushrooms 12, caps wiped and sliced into halves

Cherry tomatoes 8

Walnuts 16, roasted

Cashews 16, roasted

Hazelnuts 16, roasted

Mint leaves a handful

Dressing

Sweet basil leaves a handful

Freshly ground black pepper a pinch

Salt $^1/_2$ tsp

White onion 1, large, peeled and chopped

Pickles (gherkins) 150g ($5^1/_3$ oz)

Capers 1 tsp

Dijon mustard 1 Tbsp

Whole grain mustard 1 tsp

Wasabi to taste

Lemon juice 2 Tbsp

Olive oil 1 Tbsp

Honey 2 Tbsp

Lemon grass 2.5-cm (1-in) length, hard outer leaves removed and finely chopped

1 Combine all ingredients, except those for dressing, in a mixing bowl. Toss well and set aside.

2 Prepare dressing. Place ingredients in a blender and blend into a fine paste.

3 Pour dressing over mixed ingredients and toss well. Served garnished with mint leaves.

Rice and Noodles

A star item in most Thai restaurants, this dish cradles many flavours from seafood to beef with a whole range of spices in harmony. Thin rice vermicelli is variously known as rice noodles or string noodles. When deep-fried they swell up to become crispy, crunchy skeins that make a perfect bland foil for richly sauced meats and seafood.

Crispy Noodles Mee Krob

Serves 4

Cooking oil for deep-frying

Thin rice vermicelli 300 g (10^1/$_2$ oz), chopped into 5-cm (2-in) lengths

Garlic 2 cloves, peeled and finely chopped

Crabmeat 150 g (5^1/$_3$ oz)

Prawns (shrimps) 250 g (9 oz), peeled and deveined

Spring onions (scallions) 3, cut into 2.5-cm (1-in) lengths

Northern chilli paste (page 42) 2 Tbsp

Fish sauce 2 Tbsp

Coriander leaves (cilantro) 1 sprig, coarsely chopped

Lime juice 2 Tbsp

Sugar 1 tsp

Bean sprouts 200 g (7 oz), tailed and blanched

1   Heat oil in a wok over medium heat. Deep-fry rice vermicelli in handfuls, until vermicelli puffs up and turns light brown in colour. Remove, drain and set aside. Reserve 2 Tbsp oil.

2   Heat reserved oil over medium heat. Stir-fry garlic until fragrant. Add crabmeat, prawns and spring onions. Stir-fry for 3 minutes, or until crabmeat and prawns are cooked.

3   Add chilli paste, fish sauce, lime juice and sugar and stir well. Return fried vermicelli to the wok, add bean sprouts and toss well.

4   Serve immediately.

Given Thailand's close ties with China, both historically and geographically, noodles form an integral part of most meals. Rice noodles come either fresh or dried. The latter come in two forms, rice sticks or thin vermicelli, both needing to be blanched briefly in boiling water to reconstitute. Fresh noodles can be used as they are.

Fried Rice Noodles with Beef Kuay Teow Neau Sarn

Serves 4

Vegetable oil 3 Tbsp

Garlic 2 cloves, peeled and finely chopped

Ginger 2.5-cm (1-cm) knob, peeled and minced

Beef sirloin 250 g (9 oz), finely sliced

Fresh rice noodles 300 g (10½ oz)

Bean sprouts 100 g (3½ oz), tailed

Seasoning

Dark soy sauce 2 Tbsp

Oyster sauce 2 Tbsp

Sesame oil 1 Tbsp

Coarse black pepper 1 tsp

Water 4 Tbsp

1 Heat oil over medium heat. Stir-fry garlic and ginger until fragrant.

2 Increase heat and add beef. Stir-fry for 2 minutes. Add rice noodles, bean sprouts and seasoning ingredients and stir-fry for another 2 minutes. Add water and stir-fry until water is absorbed.

3 Serve hot, with chilli sauce on the side.

SAM LEONG

Ever a master of fusion food, Sam has integrated 2 vastly different cuisines (Japanese and Thai) to produce a culinary masterpiece. Green tea noodles are available in specialist Japanese stores and some Chinese stores. A fairly recent innovation, they have a faint, smoky flavour from the infusion of tea. Served up in a fragrant, scented green curry broth, this dish is sublime. There is no reasonable substitute for green tea noodles, but spinach noodles will pass muster–just.

Green Tea Noodles in Green Curry Broth
Kway Teow Gaeng Khiaw Wan

Green tea noodles 55 g (2 oz)

Shiitake mushrooms 4

Crabmeat 2 Tbsp, cooked and shredded

Hot water 250 ml (8 fl oz / 1 cup)

Spring onion (scallion) 1, finely chopped

Nori (seaweed) 1/2 sheet, cut into thin strips

Sweet basil leaves 1 small sprig

Seasoning

* Chicken consommé 180 ml (6 fl oz / 3/4 cup)

Lemon grass 1 stalk, hard outer leaves removed, bruised and coarsely chopped

Bird's eye chillies 2, finely chopped

Salt 1 tsp

Green curry paste (page 41) 1 Tbsp

---

* Chicken consommé

Makes about 2 litres (64 fl oz / 8 cups). Any excess stock can be kept refrigerated for up to 1 week or frozen for up to 3 months. Use as needed.

Water 4 litres (128 fl oz / 16 cups)

Chicken 1 kg (2 lb 3 oz)

Lean pork 750 g (1 lb 10 oz)

Chinese (Yunnan) ham 330 g (12 oz)

Bring water to the boil in a large stockpot. Add chicken, pork and ham. Reduce heat and simmer for 8 hours, or until only about 2 litres (64 fl oz / 8 cups) stock is left. Strain stock and discard chicken, pork and ham.

---

1 Bring a pot of water to the boil. Add noodles and cook for 2 minutes, or until just tender. Drain, place noodles in a serving bowl and set aside.

2 Poach mushrooms in hot water for 3 minutes and drain. Arrange together with crabmeat on top of noodles.

3 Prepare seasoning. Bring chicken consommé to the boil over medium heat. Add lemon grass, chillies, salt and green curry paste. Stir well to blend. Remove from heat and gently pour over noodles.

4 Serve immediately, garnished with spring onion, seaweed and basil leaves.

VATCHARIN BHUMICHITR

When Vatch went on to carve an impressive career extolling Thai cuisine instead of continuing his printing career, it was the printing world's loss and the food world's gain. Vatch's efforts in importing the hitherto esoteric ingredients such as galangal, lime leaves and sweet basil certainly gave me a frisson of excitement when I ran my first restaurant.

Thai, Singapore, Malaysian, Indonesian and all the Indo-Chinese cuisines share much the same cultural heritage. Many of the ingredients cross over the countries; but for the different names, dishes such as these stir-fried noodles are fairly similar. But given the Thai penchant for chilli heat, there is usually more than a soupçon of the pod whatever is cooked.

Stir-fried Noodles with Prawns and Dried Chillies Kuay Teow Phad Gung

Serves 2

Cooking oil 2 Tbsp

Garlic 2 cloves, peeled and finely chopped

Ginger 2.5-cm (1-in) knob, peeled and finely chopped

Dried chilli 1, large, coarsely chopped

King prawns (shrimps) 4, peeled and deveined, leaving heads and tails intact

Onion 1, medium, peeled and finely chopped

Wheat flour noodles 250 g (9 oz), soaked to soften and drained

Fish sauce 1 Tbsp

Light soy sauce 1 Tbsp

Sugar 1 tsp

Coriander leaves (cilantro) a handful, coarsely chopped

1 Heat oil in a wok over medium heat. Stir-fry garlic until fragrant, then add ginger and chilli. Stir-fry for 1 minute.

2 Add prawns and stir-fry until prawns change colour and are cooked. Add onion, fish sauce, soy sauce and sugar and stir-fry for 1 minute. Add noodles and toss well.

3 Serve garnished with coriander leaves.

BLUE ELEPHANT COOKERY SCHOOL (RUNGSAN MULIJAN [CHANG])

When the Belgian owner of the Blue Elephant Group decided to open a cookery school, it sent a ripple of excitement among foodies. Headed by Chang and backed up by his team of dazzling chefs who have seen to the mechanics and semantics of the cuisine here at the school-cum-restaurant, this has become a culinary landmark.

Black spaghetti is, curiously enough, an Italian staple, but it is making many inroads into Thai and even Japanese cooking. It derives its colour from squid ink and looks, if a little strange, still very appetising.

Black Spaghetti Phad Kee Maow

Serves 1

Sweet basil leaves 15

Olive oil 3 Tbsp

Seafood (prawns [shrimps], squid tubes, mussels and scallops) 500 g (1 lb 1^1/$_2$ oz), washed and cleaned

Cod fillet 100 g (3^1/$_2$ oz), cut into thick slices and coated in plain (all-purpose) flour

Black spaghetti 100 g (3^1/$_2$ oz), cooked until al dente

Chicken stock or water 3 Tbsp

Fish sauce ^{1}/$_2$ Tbsp

Light soy sauce 1 tsp

Sugar ^{1}/$_2$ tsp

Kaffir lime leaf 1

Green peppercorns 1 tsp

Red chilli 1, seeded and finely sliced into strips

Tomato sauce

Tomatoes 3

Olive oil 1 tsp

Butter 1 tsp

White onion 1, peeled and finely diced

Garlic 2 cloves, peeled and finely chopped

Salt ^{1}/$_2$ tsp

Sugar ^{1}/$_2$ tsp

Ground white pepper ^{1}/$_2$ tsp

Chicken stock or water 2 Tbsp

Sweet basil leaves 10

Chilli paste

Red or orange chilli 1, finely sliced

Bird's eye chillies 5, finely chopped

Garlic 2 cloves, peeled and finely sliced

1 Prepare tomato sauce. Bring a pot of water to the boil and blanch tomatoes for 30 seconds. Remove and quickly plunge into a basin of iced water for 1–2 minutes. Peel and discard skins. Cut tomatoes in half, scoop out seeds and cut into small pieces. Set aside.

2 Heat olive oil in a saucepan over medium heat. Add butter and stir-fry white onion and garlic for 3 minutes, or until fragrant. Add tomatoes, salt, sugar, pepper and stock or water. Stir-fry for 2 minutes. Add basil leaves, stir well for 10 seconds and remove mixture from heat. Using a blender, blend mixture until smooth. Set aside.

3 Prepare chilli paste. Using a mortar and pestle, combine chillies and garlic and pound into a fine paste.

4 Heat olive oil in a wok over medium heat. Fry basil leaves for 3–5 minutes, or until crisp. Remove, drain and set aside. Reserve oil.

5 Reheat oil over medium heat. Add chilli paste and stir-fry until fragrant. Add seafood and cod fillet and stir-fry for 2 minutes, or until well cooked.

6 Add spaghetti and toss well. Stir-fry for 1 minute.

7 Add tomato sauce, stock or water, fish sauce, soy sauce, sugar, kaffir lime leaf and peppercorns and stir-fry for 1 minute.

8 Serve immediately, garnished with fried basil leaves and red chilli strips.

RUJIREKA SOUWAPAWONG

Reka does not elaborate on the "millionaire" description; suffice that it has supreme flavour and probably a much-loved dish. It is a rich compendium of succulent noodles, aromatic seasoning with a tangy crunch from the spring onions and ground peanuts. "Set tee" means millionaire in Thai and has nothing to do with something you sit on!

Millionaire Noodles Kway Teow Set Tee

Serves 2

Vegetable oil 1 Tbsp

Garlic 2 cloves, peeled and finely chopped

Prawns (shrimps) 4, medium, peeled and deveined

Chicken breast 55 g (2 oz), sliced

Lean pork 55 g (2 oz), sliced

Fish sauce 1 Tbsp

Bean sprouts 100 g (3½ oz), tailed and blanched

Fresh rice noodles 250 g (9 oz)

Sugar 1 tsp

Spring onion (scallion) 1, chopped into 4-cm (1.5-in) lengths

Roasted peanuts 1 Tbsp, ground

Coriander leaves (cilantro) a handful, coarsely chopped

1 Heat oil over high heat. Stir-fry garlic until fragrant, then add prawns, chicken, pork and fish sauce. Stir-fry for 5–7 minutes.

2 Add bean sprouts and rice noodles, sugar and spring onions. Stir-fry until well mixed.

3 Dish out and serve garnished with peanuts and coriander leaves.

Ubiquitous throughout Thailand, this dish is the most basic form of fried noodles and is typically Thai in the use of chopped or ground peanuts for garnish. There are several variations, depending on which part of Thailand it comes from. Some are light and others spicy. This one has just the hint of chilli.

Fried Rice Noodles with Chicken Phad Thai Gai

Serves 4

Vegetable oil 3 Tbsp

Garlic 2 cloves, peeled and finely chopped

Chicken breast 250 g (8 oz), cut into thin slices

Bean sprouts 200 g (7 oz), tailed

Fresh rice noodles 300 g (10½ oz)

Fish sauce 2 Tbsp

Dark soy sauce 2 Tbsp

Lime juice 1 Tbsp

Chilli powder 1 tsp

Water 3 Tbsp

Roasted peanuts a handful, chopped

1 Heat oil over medium heat. Stir-fry garlic for 2 minutes, or until fragrant. Increase heat. Add chicken and stir-fry for 3 minutes, or until chicken is cooked.

2 Add bean sprouts, noodles, fish sauce, soy sauce, lime juice and chilli powder. Toss well and stir-fry for 2 minutes. Add water and stir-fry for another 2 minutes.

3 Dish out and serve garnished with chopped peanuts.

If there ever is one dish that typifies Thai street food, it is this all-in-one noodle meal redolent with savoury stock, chicken, crunchy bean sprouts and, for good measure, a spicy dip of chillies, fish sauce and lime juice. Fresh rice noodles are sold in most Chinese supermarkets, but dried rice sticks are good substitutes that need only to be blanched in boiling water for a few minutes. If using the latter, half the weight specified is sufficient for one portion as dry noodles double in bulk when cooked.

Rice Noodle Soup Kway Teow Gai

Serves 2

Water 800 ml (26 fl oz /3¼ cups)

Chicken stock cube 1

Fish sauce 2 Tbsp

Chicken breast 200 g (7 oz)

Ground black pepper ½ tsp

Bean sprouts 100 g (3½ oz), tailed and blanched

Coriander leaves (cilantro) 1 sprig, coarsely chopped

Fresh rice noodles 300 g (10½ oz)

Dipping sauce

Red chillies 2, finely chopped

Fish sauce 2 Tbsp

Lime juice 1 Tbsp

1 Bring water to the boil over medium heat. Add stock cube and fish sauce and stir well. Add chicken and cook for 10 minutes, or until chicken changes colour and is cooked. Remove, drain and set aside to cool.

2 Return stock to the boil. Add pepper. Reduce heat and leave to simmer until ready to serve. Meanwhile, finely shred chicken breast and divide into 2 portions. Divide noodles into 2 portions and place in serving bowls. Top noodles with chicken and bean sprouts.

3 Prepare dipping sauce. Combine ingredients and mix well. Set aside.

4 Ladle stock over noodles. Serve immediately, garnished with coriander leaves and with dipping sauce on the side.

Tip: Use prawns or squid in place of chicken, or mushrooms as a vegetarian option if desired. If fresh rice noodles are not available, use 150 g (5⅓ oz) dry rice sticks, cooked in boiling water for 6–8 minutes.

How this dish became entrenched within Malaysia and Singapore is the stuff of culinary revolution. There is no identical creation in Thailand, principally because this was 'borrowed' by the two neighbouring countries. "Mee" simply means noodle in Malay, which is a phonetic tweak from the Chinese "mian". So there you have it, a glorious pastiche of rice noodles, spices and a gravy heavy with Chinese yellow beans.

Mee Siam Mee Kati

Serves 6–8

Dried rice vermicelli 400 g (14⅓ oz)

Vegetable oil 3 Tbsp

Dried prawns (shrimps) 4 Tbsp, soaked, drained and finely ground

Bean sprouts 150 g (5⅓ oz), tailed

Chinese (garlic) chives 70 g (2½ oz), cut into 4-cm (1½-in) lengths

Prawns (shrimps) 350 g (12 oz), peeled and deveined

Red curry paste (page 39) 2 Tbsp

Hard-boiled eggs 4, peeled and sliced

Lime 4, small, cut into wedges

Gravy

Coconut milk 250 ml (8 fl oz / 1 cup)

Tamarind paste 3 Tbsp, mixed with 750 ml (24 fl oz / 3 cups) water and strained

Fermented yellow bean sauce 3 Tbsp

Red curry paste (page 39) 2 Tbsp

Onion 1, large, peeled and finely chopped

Salt 2 tsp

Sugar 2 tsp

1 Prepare gravy. Combine ingredients and simmer over low heat for 10 minutes, or until onion is soft and translucent.

2 Soak vermicelli in hot water for 5–7 minutes, drain and set aside.

3 Heat oil in a wok over medium heat. Stir-fry dried prawns for 3 minutes, then add bean sprouts, chives (reserve some for garnish), prawns and vermicelli. Stir-fry for 3 minutes, or until prawns are cooked. Add curry paste and stir-fry for another 2 minutes, or until well mixed.

4 Divide noodles into serving portions of approximately 150 g (5⅓ oz) each. Ladle enough gravy to moisten noodles over each portion.

5 Serve immediately, garnished with hard-boiled egg slices, lime wedges and reserved chives.

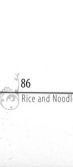

KEN HOM

I am often bemused (and a little delighted) when mistaken for Ken at the various food shows where I demonstrate Southeast Asian cooking, by virtue of the both of us being Chinese. Ken's television appearances are what I watch avidly, for there is much one can learn from his kitchen technique and talents.

Green Rice is nothing short of cutting edge Chinese cuisine. It certainly rings a nice hybrid change from the basic grain and may well become a talking point when you serve it at a dinner party.

Green Rice Khao Pad Ja

Serves 4-6

Water 900 ml (30 fl oz / 3¹/₂ cups)

Long grain rice 400 g (14¹/₃ oz)

Peanut oil 1 Tbsp

 Garlic 1 Tbsp, peeled and coarsely chopped

Coriander leaves (cilantro) 1 sprig, finely chopped

Spring onions (scallions) 2, finely chopped

Frozen green peas 250 g (8 oz), thawed at room
    temperature

Salt 2 tsp

1 Prepare rice 1 day in advance. Bring water to the boil. Add rice and boil for 10 minutes, or until steam holes appear on surface of rice. Reduce heat and simmer for 15 minutes. Drain any excess liquid. Allow rice to cool thoroughly, cover in plastic wrap (cling) film and refrigerate until use.

2 Heat oil in a wok over medium heat. Stir-fry garlic for 10 seconds, then add rice and stir-fry for 3 minutes, or until thoroughly heated through. Add coriander, spring onions, peas and salt. Stir-fry for 2 minutes.

3 Dish out and serve immediately.

Mung bean noodles are also known as translucent vermicelli or glass noodles. A remarkable characteristic of these noodles is that they can be cooked for a long time without turning mushy. It is the kind of noodles that gets tossed into salads, stir-fries and other dishes because of their resilient quality. Crunchy and smooth at the same time, it is a treat.

Mung Bean Noodles with Crabmeat Puu Phad Woon Sen

Serves 4

Vegetable oil 3 Tbsp

Garlic 2 cloves, peeled and minced

Ginger 2.5-cm (1-in) knob, peeled and minced

Mung bean noodles 300 g (10¹/₂ oz), soaked to soften, then drained

Fish sauce 2 Tbsp

Ground black pepper 1 tsp

Spring onions (scallions) 2, finely chopped

Sweet basil leaves a handful, coarsely chopped

Crabmeat 400 g (14 oz), cooked

Water 90 ml (3 fl oz / 1³/₈ cup)

Red chillies 3, finely chopped

1 Heat oil in a wok over medium heat. Stir-fry garlic and ginger for 1 minute, or until fragrant. Add noodles, fish sauce, pepper, spring onions and basil. Stir-fry for 2 minutes, or until well mixed.

2 Add crabmeat and water. Stir-fry for 2 minutes, or until most of the water is absorbed.

3 Dish out and serve garnished with chillies.

This is one of my all-time favourites and cuts a real dash when served in a scooped out pineapple half, a real pièce de résistance. It is a rich assemblage of choice ingredients that complement the blandness of rice and cuts a sharp, sweet dash with juicy pineapple chunks. It is believed to have originated from the Thai Royal kitchens. When in season, there is a type of small Thai pineapple the size of a grapefruit, called golden pineapple, that is positively ambrosial. Use if available.

Pineapple Rice Khao Phad

Serves 4

Pineapple 1, medium

Vegetable oil 3 Tbsp

Garlic 2 cloves, peeled and finely chopped

Shallots 2 Tbsp, peeled and finely chopped

Eggs 3

Prawns (shrimps) 200 g (7 oz), peeled

Cooked jasmine rice 400 g (14 oz)

Fish sauce 2 Tbsp

Red chillies 2, finely chopped

Spring onion (scallion) 1, finely chopped

Vegetable stock or water 90 ml (3 fl oz / ³/₈ cup)

Coriander leaves (cilantro) a handful

1 Cut pineapple into halves vertically. Scoop out flesh, cut into cubes and set aside.

2 Heat oil in a wok over medium heat. Stir-fry garlic and shallots for 2 minutes, or until fragrant.

3 Break eggs into wok and cook for a minute. Add prawns and stir-fry for 2 minutes, or until prawns change colour and are cooked. Increase heat. Add diced pineapple, rice, fish sauce, chillies, spring onion and vegetable stock or water. Stir-fry for 3 minutes, or until stock is absorbed.

4 Ladle rice into pineapple shells. Serve garnished with coriander leaves.

RUJIREKA SOUWAPAWONG

*This is a hearty dish steeped in the rustic tradition of Thai village lifestyles. Many Thais eat fried rice for breakfast, provided it is not too heavy or spicy. Try to get hold of Thai anchovies, such as the King fish anchovy (*pla in see kem*) as they are less oily.*

Anchovy Fried Rice Khao Phad Pla Kem

Serves 2

Vegetable oil 1 Tbsp

Garlic 1 clove, peeled and finely chopped

Thai anchovy or salted fish 1–2, diced

Red bird's eye chillies 2, finely chopped

Fish sauce 1 Tbsp

Cooked white rice 250 g (9 oz), chilled

Spring onion (scallion) 1, finely chopped

Coriander leaves (cilantro) 1 sprig, finely chopped

Lime 1, small, cut into wedges

1 Heat oil in a wok over medium heat. Stir-fry garlic until fragrant. Add anchovy or salted fish, chillies, fish sauce and rice. Use a spatula to break up any lumps of rice. Stir-fry ingredients until well mixed and heated through.

2 Dish out and serve hot, garnished with spring onion, coriander and lime wedges on the side.

Tip: Anchovies can be substituted with any other meat, fish or seafood. As an extra treat, fry an egg, sunny-side-up style for each portion and place on top of rice before serving.

Poultry

VATCHRIN BHUMICHITR

While a sterling ambassador for the cuisine of his country, Vatch is equally adept when it comes to interpreting those of his Asian neighbours. Many a meal I have had at his latest eatery, Southeast W9 in London's chic Maida Vale gave cause for admiration. He has certainly not taken a leaf from my culinary heritage in vain, and his menu cuts a delicious swathe across Thailand, Laos, Kampuchea, Vietnam, Myanmar, Malaysia and Singapore.

This is an extremely simple salad to prepare, that will also garner many compliments. Mint is an underrated herb, but the Thais know how to coax every drop of its tangy perfume. There is an intriguing harmony between mint, lime juice, fish sauce and chillies that really comes through in the dressing.

Chicken Salad with Mint and Nuts Yam Gai

Serves 4

Chicken breasts 180 g (6 oz), skinned

Bean sprouts 85 g (3 oz), tailed

Cucumber 2, cut into halves, seeded and cut into 5-cm (2-in) lengths

Red onion 2, peeled and finely sliced

Bird's eye chillies 2, finely chopped

Fish sauce 2 Tbsp

Lime juice 2 Tbsp

Mint leaves a handful, finely chopped

Roasted peanuts 2 Tbsp, finely ground

Roasted sesame seeds 2 Tbsp

1 Bring a pot of water to the boil. Add chicken and boil until chicken changes colour and is cooked. Remove, drain and set aside to cool.

2 Shred chicken and place in a mixing bowl. Add all other ingredients and toss well before serving.

This is one of Isaan's most famous dishes that has tickled taste buds around the world. It seems like street food gone posh, or it can take on the guise of a royal dish depending on who cooks it. So ubiquitous is it today that gai yang can be had from the peripatetic streets of Bangkok to the beaches of Phuket. As one of the most delicious ways to cook chicken, it lends itself to endless variations of spicing. This is my personal and perennial favourite.

Grilled Chicken Gai Yang

Serves 4

Chicken legs 4, large

Vegetable oil 2 Tbsp

Marinade

Ground black pepper 1 Tbsp

Garlic 2 cloves, peeled and minced

Galangal 1-cm ($^1/_2$-in) knob, peeled and minced

Coriander leaves (cilantro) 1 sprig, finely chopped

Fish sauce 2 Tbsp

Honey 1 Tbsp

Lime juice 2 Tbsp

1 Prepare marinade. Combine ingredients for marinade in a mixing bowl and mix well. Place chicken in to steep in the marinade and set aside in a cool place for 1 hour.

2 Place chicken in a preheated oven at 220°C (440°F), or over a grill for 20 minutes. Baste chicken with oil every 5 minutes, turning it over each time, until skin is slightly charred.

3 Serve hot, with a dip (page 43).

Barbecues are very much a universal mode of cooking, even if referred to in different terms by different countries. In Thailand and most of tropical Asia, charcoal grilling, as it is called, is a fundamental and age-old Asian mode of cooking. Call it alfresco or whatever; cooking outdoors has been an Asian practice for centuries given the tropical heat. The result of barbecued chicken marinated with ingredients such as light soy sauce, lime juice, kaffir lime leaves and chilli is fragrant and mouth-watering. This marinade is typically Thai and serves well as a dip, when boiled briefly.

Chilli Chicken Gai BBQ

Serves 4

Chicken breasts 4, skinned and cleaned

Lemon grass 1 stalk, tough outer leaves removed; root end bruised

Vegetable oil 2 Tbsp

Water 3 Tbsp

Marinade

Light soy sauce 2 Tbsp

Kaffir lime leaves 4, finely shredded

Red chilli 1, finely chopped

Garlic 2 cloves, peeled and minced

Lime juice 3 Tbsp

Sugar 2 tsp

1 Prepare marinade. Combine all marinade ingredients in a mixing bowl and mix well.

2 Score chicken with a few deep cuts and place in marinade to steep for 1–2 hours. Remove chicken and pour marinade into a pot. Set aside.

3 Place chicken in a preheated oven at 220°C (440°F), or over a grill for 10–15 minutes. Dip bruised lemon grass in oil and baste chicken every 5 minutes, turning it over each time.

4 Meanwhile, prepare dipping sauce for chicken. Add water to marinade and mix well. Bring to the boil for 5 minutes and pour into a sauce dish.

5 Serve chicken hot, with dipping sauce on the side.

KEN HOM

What this man does not know about Chinese cuisine you can fit into Tom Thumb's thimble. Ken is practically a culinary icon popping up here, there and everywhere on television, at many august establishments like the Oriental Bangkok, on the regal Queen Elizabeth II and others too numerous to mention here.

I particularly like this dish and given that kiwi fruit is not exactly mainstream Thai, this dish is about employing one's culinary ingenuity. The fruit's tart sweetness cuts the savoury flavour of chicken very nicely. Hybrids can indeed be pleasurable culinary experiences!

Stir-fried Kiwi Chicken Gai Phad Kiwi

Serves 4–6

Chicken breasts 450 g (1 lb), skinned and fat trimmed

Corn flour (cornstarch) 1 tsp

Salt 1 tsp

Peanut oil 1 Tbsp

Garlic 2 cloves, peeled and finely chopped

Chilli bean sauce 1 tsp

Sugar 1 tsp

Kiwi fruit 2, peeled and diced

Sesame oil 1 tsp

1 Dice chicken into 1-cm (¹/₂-in) cubes and place in a mixing bowl. Add corn flour and salt and coat chicken evenly.

2 Heat oil in a wok over medium heat. Stir-fry garlic until fragrant. Add chicken and stir-fry for 5–7 minutes, or until chicken changes colour and is cooked.

3 Add chilli bean sauce, sugar and kiwi fruit. Stir-fry for 1 minute, then add sesame oil and mix well.

4 Dish out and serve immediately.

Tip: If unavailable, kiwi fruit can be substituted with mango and papaya.

Thais rarely cook chicken off the bone, as the marrow provides an extra flavour. This is wonderfully fragrant curry that, despite minimal preparation, does not compromise or lack in flavour, as the chicken parts are seared to seal the juices in.

Chicken and Lemon Grass Curry Gaeng Gai Takrai

Serves 4

Chicken 1, about 1.5 kg (3 lb 4^1/$_2$ oz), skinned,
fat trimmed and cleaned

Cooking oil 2 Tbsp

Lemon grass 2 stalks, tough outer leaves
removed and finely sliced

Onion 1, large, peeled and sliced

Coconut milk 500 ml (16 fl oz / 2 cups)

Tamarind juice 1 Tbsp paste, mixed with 125 ml
(4 fl oz / ^{1}/$_2$ cup) water and strained

Palm sugar 1 Tbsp

Red curry paste (page 39) 1 Tbsp

1 Cut chicken into 6–8 pieces. Heat oil in a pan over high heat. Sear chicken parts for
3 minutes. Remove, drain and set aside. Reserve oil.

2 Heat reserved oil over medium heat. Stir-fry lemon grass and onion for 2 minutes, or until
fragrant. Add coconut milk, tamarind juice, palm sugar and curry paste. Stir well. Reduce
heat and simmer for 5 minutes.

3 Return chicken to the pan. Stir well and simmer for 30 minutes, or until chicken is tender.

4 Dish out and serve immediately.

The name of this dish is derived from the island of Penang off the west coast of Malaysia, and it is one of the triumvirate–the other two being gaeng phed (hot curry) and gaeng khiaw wan (green curry)–that exemplify the central Thai preference for strong, rich flavours. Many dishes of the region come under the influence of Malaysian cooking styles and this speaks of the bond between the two schools of cooking.

Penang Chicken Curry Gaeng Paneang Gai

Serves 4

Coconut milk 300 ml (10 fl oz /1¼ cups)

Red curry paste (page 39) 2 Tbsp

Cooking oil 1 Tbsp

Red chillies 2, seeded and finely sliced

Lemon grass 2 stalks, tough outer leaves removed and bruised

Tomatoes 4, sliced into quarters

Kaffir lime leaves 6

Tomato purée 1 Tbsp

Fish sauce 2 Tbsp

Lime juice 2 Tbsp

Chicken breast 450 g (1 lb), cut into thick slices

1 Combine coconut milk and red curry paste in a pot. Bring to the boil for 5 minutes, stirring constantly. Remove from heat and set aside.

2 Heat oil in a wok over medium heat. Stir-fry chillies, lemon grass, tomatoes and kaffir lime leaves for 2 minutes, or until fragrant.

3 Add coconut and curry mixture, tomato purée, fish sauce, lime juice and chicken. Stir well and simmer for 20 minutes, uncovered, or until liquid is reduced to less than half of original amount.

4 Dish out and serve garnished with sliced red chillies, if desired.

CHIANG MAI COOKERY SCHOOL (SOMPAN NABNIAN)

In the months leading up to my trip to Chiang Mai, my anticipation knew no bounds and when I visited the Chiang Mai Cookery sShool, it touched my foodie soul. Situated about half an hour form downtown Chiang Mai in Moon Muang Road, it is a heady oasis of exotic ambience. It is with joy that one grabs handfuls of lime leaves, screwpine (toei) leaves and lemon grass from the earth next to one's wok station! Sompan says this dish reminds him of his childhood when his mother would often cook this northern curry.

The resultant sauce has an unusual texture due to the inclusion of ground, roasted glutinous rice and can be made using whatever selection of vegetables you have available. Glutinous rice is a daily staple of Thailand's north and northeast regions. An extremely starchy grain when cooked, it lends itself very well to eating au natural, with fingers doing the service instead of forks and spoons or chopsticks.

Mixed Vegetable Curry with Chicken Gaeng Kae Gai

Serves 4

Glutinous (sticky) rice 100 g (3$^{1}/_{2}$ oz)

Oil 4 Tbsp

Red curry paste (page 39) 4 Tbsp

Chicken breast 300 g (10$^{1}/_{2}$ oz), thinly sliced

Long aubergine (eggplant/brinjal) 1, large, cut into 1-cm ($^{1}/_{2}$-in) lengths

Apple aubergines (eggplants/brinjals) 4, cut into small pieces

Long beans 2, cut into 2-cm (1-in) lengths

Chicken stock or water 500 ml (16 fl oz / 2 cups)

Sawtooth coriander 7 leaves, roughly chopped

Fish sauce 2 Tbsp

Bay leaves a handful, roughly chopped

Red chilli 1, finely chopped

Salt $^{1}/_{2}$ tsp

1 Heat a pan over medium heat. Dry-fry glutinous rice until rice grains turn golden brown. Transfer rice grains to a mortar and pestle and ground into a fine paste. Set aside 1 Tbsp of ground rice and store remaining cooled ground rice in an airtight container for future use.

2 Heat oil in a wok over medium heat. Stir-fry curry paste for 2 minutes, or until fragrant. Add chicken and stir-fry until chicken changes colour and is cooked.

3 Add aubergines and long beans. Stir-fry for 2 minutes.

4 Add sawtooth coriander and half of chicken stock or water. Simmer for 2 minutes. Add remaining chicken stock or water, fish sauce, bay leaves and chilli. Bring mixture to the boil, then add roasted glutinous rice and salt. Stir well. Allow mixture to simmer for another 2 minutes before removing from heat.

5 Dish out and serve immediately.

This is a feature of southern Thai cooking and also reflective of Indonesian and north Malaysian influences. As southern Thailand nudges this largely Muslim region, much of the cooking has overtones of the cuisine. Yellow curries are also a close cousin of Myanmar (Burmese) ones as turmeric that gives it its characteristic colour, is a fundamental ingredient in this neighbouring country.

Yellow Chicken Curry Gaeng Kari Gai

Serves 6

Vegetable oil 4 Tbsp

Yellow curry paste (page 38) 3 Tbsp

Coconut milk 750 ml (24 fl oz / 3 cups)

Lemon grass 2 stalks, tough outer leaves removed, chopped and bruised

Kaffir lime leaves 4

Chicken drumsticks or thighs 12

Salt 2 tsp

Sugar 1 tsp

1   Heat oil in a wok over medium heat. Fry curry paste for 6 minutes. Add 2 Tbsp coconut milk and stir well. Fry for 2 minutes.

2   Add remaining coconut milk, lemon grass, kaffir lime leaves and chicken. Stir well. Reduce heat and simmer for 25 minutes.

3   Add salt and sugar. Stir well. Increase heat and simmer for 10 minutes.

4   Dish out and serve hot.

This is an unusual recipe in that no chilli is used, yet the resultant dish has a piquant bite with an elusive lemony tang from the lemon grass. It's the best introductory kind of curry to serve those not used to Thai heat.

White Chicken Gaeng Chud Gai

Serves 6

Chicken 1, about 1 kg (2 lb 3 oz), fat trimmed

Cooking oil 4 Tbsp

Coconut milk 750 ml (24 fl oz / 3 cups)

Salt 1 tsp

Lemon grass 2 stalks, tough outer leaves removed and bruised

Fish sauce 1 Tbsp

Lime 1

Paste

Onion 1, small, peeled and finely sliced

Garlic 3 cloves, peeled and finely chopped

Galangal 2.5-cm (1-in) knob, peeled and finely sliced

Ground coriander 2 Tbsp

Ground fennel 1 tsp

Ground cumin 1 Tbsp

1 Cut chicken into 8 pieces and set aside.

2 Prepare paste. Combine all ingredients for paste and place in a blender. Blend into a fine paste.

3 Heat oil in a wok over high heat. Fry paste for 5 minutes. Add 2 Tbsp coconut milk and stir well. Fry for 2 minutes.

4 Add remaining coconut milk, salt, lemon grass and fish sauce. Stir well and bring mixture to the boil. Reduce heat, then add chicken and simmer for 35–40 minutes, or until chicken is tender.

5 Dish out and squeeze lime over chicken. Serve immediately.

PHILIPPA KINGSLEY

When Philippa decamped to Atlanta, Georgia from her former home in the Hague (Dutch taste buds were never quite the same again), she did not miss a single 'fiddle dee dee' cooking Thai food in America's deep south. She pops up ever so often in local food magazines and is very active on the Board of The Thai Association of Georgia.

Roasting the bird is straightforward enough and there are various ways to do this, depending on taste. The sky will not fall if you purchase a ready-roasted duck or a portion of breast as it saves effort and time. For this, Philippa urges you to start from scratch.

Spicy Roast Duck with Crispy Noodles and Cashews Yam Pet Yang

Serves 6

Duck breasts 6

Dried egg noodles 200 g (7 oz)

Cooking oil for deep-frying

Red onion 1, peeled and finely sliced

Spring onions (scallions) 6, finely sliced

Mint leaves a handful

Coriander leaves (coriander) a handful

Unsalted roasted cashew nuts 100 g (3¹/₂ oz)

Marinade

Lime juice 250 ml (8 fl oz / 1 cup)

Northern chilli paste (page 42) 8 Tbsp

Fish sauce 3 Tbsp

Dark brown sugar 1 Tbsp

1 Wash duck breasts, then pat dry with paper towels.

2 Pre-heat oven to 250°C (475°F) for 15 minutes. Fill a deep baking dish with 625 ml (20 fl oz /2¹/₂ cups) cold water. Place a roasting rack over baking dish and arrange duck breasts on top. Roast duck for 20–30 minutes. Duck meat should be cooked to medium-well doneness. Remove and leave to cool. Cut into thin slices.

3 Combine ingredients for marinade in a mixing bowl and mix well. Place duck slices in to steep in the marinade for 1 hour, then drain and set aside for 1 hour. Drain and set aside.

4 Separate noodle strands, using your hands to break them up into short lengths. Heat oil over medium heat and deep-fry noodles until crisp and golden brown. Remove and drain well.

5 Arrange crispy noodles on a serving dish and arrange marinated duck slices on top. Serve garnished with red onion, spring onions, mint and coriander leaves and cashew nuts.

Deceptively simple, this rich duck dish takes on an incredible flavour when married with tamarind and palm sugar, two Thai ingredients that have remarkable compatibility. The important thing is to cook the bird long and slow, at least an hour and a half, before the meat becomes fork-tender and the sauce takes on a rich gloss.

Braised Duck in Tamarind and Coriander Pet See Yiew Tun Pak Chee

Serves 6

Ground coriander 3 Tbsp

Salt 2 Tbsp

Ground black pepper 2 tsp

Palm sugar 2 Tbsp

Dark soy sauce 4 Tbsp

Duck 1, about 2.5 kg (5 lb 8 oz), giblets and
    excess fat removed, washed and dried

Vegetable oil 250 ml (8 fl oz / 1 cup)

Spanish onion 1, large, peeled and
    finely chopped

Water 2 litres (64 fl oz / 8 cups)

Tamarind juice 4 Tbsp paste, mixed with 6 Tbsp
    water and strained

Cinnamon stick 8-cm (3-in) length

Cloves 8

Coriander leaves (cilantro) 3 sprigs,
    coarsely chopped

1 Add coriander, salt, pepper, sugar and soy sauce to a large mixing bowl and mix well. Place duck in to steep in the marinade and set aside in a cool place for an hour.

2 Heat oil in a large wok over high heat. Fry onion for 5 minutes, or until soft.

3 Place duck in wok and fry using a spatula to scoop and drizzle oil over body for 10 minutes, or until the skin turns crisp and brown.

4 Add water, tamarind juice, cinnamon and cloves. Reduce heat, cover wok and leave to simmer for 2 hours, or until flesh is tender. If necessary, add more water.

5 Remove lid from wok and increase heat to reduce liquid by half. Remove duck from heat and set aside to cool before slicing into pieces. Reserve any excess liquid for serving as a dipping sauce.

6 Serve garnished with coriander leaves.

KHUN SUNANT WILIARAT (MADAM PA)

The use of star anise and cinnamon echoes Thailand's ancient Indian ties when the country was a largely Hindu enclave, all of 3,000 years ago. By bathing the duck in an aromatic and subtle tamarind sauce that cuts the bird's fat in the sweetest way, Madam Pa does something quite extraordinary.

Duck with Tamarind Sauce Pet Nam Makarm

Serves 4

Cooking oil 8 Tbsp

Chopped shallots 1 tsp

Dried chillies 2, chopped

Lean duck breast 180 g (6^1/$_2$ oz), sliced

Salad greens

Marinade

Coriander seeds 1 Tbsp

Star anise 1

Cinnamon stick 2.5-cm (1-in) length

Garlic 1 clove, peeled and finely chopped

Coriander (cilantro) leaves 1 sprig

Light soy sauce 2 tsp

Sauce

Water 4 Tbsp

Palm sugar 180 g (6^1/$_2$ oz)

Fish sauce 2 tsp

Light soy sauce 125 ml (4 fl oz / ^{1}/$_2$ cup)

Tamarind juice 2 Tbsp paste, mixed with 250 ml (8 fl oz /1 cup) and strained

Corn flour (cornstarch) 3 Tbsp, mixed with 6 Tbsp water

1   Heat oil in a wok over medium heat. Deep-fry shallots and dried chillies separately, until crisp. Remove, drain and set aside.

2   Prepare marinade. Preheat an oven to 180°C (350°F). Place coriander seeds, star anise and cinnamon on a baking tray and roast for 10 minutes. Remove from oven and place into a mortar with garlic and coriander leaves. Pound ingredients until fine. Transfer to a mixing bowl, add light soy sauce and mix well. Place duck slices in to steep in the marinade and and set aside in a cool place for 1 hour.

3   Heat a grill pan over medium heat, or preheat an oven to 220°C (440°F). Grill marinated duck slices for 4 minutes on each side to desired doneness.

4   Prepare sauce. Combine all sauce ingredients except corn flour mixture and bring to the boil. Stir in corn flour mixture until sauce thickens.

5   Arrange duck slices on a serving plate and drizzle sauce over. Serve garnished with deep-fried shallots and dried chillies.

How well I remember eating soy sauce braised goose in Bangkok's food centre, Ma Boon Khong. Given that this bird is not easily available, duck is a good substitute with a similar richness. It is a classic of the Teo Chew *community. It takes time to cook this dish, but the taste is well worth the effort.*

Soy Braised Duck Pet See Yiew

Serves 6

Vegetable oil 2 Tbsp

Sugar 2 Tbsp

Duck 1, about 2 kg (4 lb 6 oz), giblets and excess fat removed, washed and dried

Corn flour (cornstarch) 2 tsp, mixed with 2 Tbsp water

Cucumber 1, peeled and thinly sliced

Braising liquid

Dark soy sauce 5 Tbsp

Galangal 5-cm (2-in) knob, peeled and chopped

Spring onions (scallions) 4, chopped

Five-spice powder 2 tsp

Salt 2 tsp

Water 2.5 litres (80 fl oz / 10 cups)

1 Heat oil in a large wok over medium heat. Add sugar and caramelise until sugar turns frothy and dark brown. Place duck in wok. Using a spatula, scoop caramelised sugar over duck and coat evenly.

2 Prepare braising liquid. Combine all ingredients and add to wok. Cover and allow duck to simmer for 2 hours, or until duck is tender. Remove duck from heat and set aside to cool before slicing. Reserve braising liquid.

3 Prepare dipping sauce. Strain reserved braising liquid into a pot. Bring to the boil over high heat for 15 minutes, then add corn flour mixture and stir until thickened. Pour into a sauce dish.

4 Serve duck with sliced cucumber and dipping sauce on the side.

This dish is believed to have hailed originally from the Sichuan province, but is now firmly entrenched within the ranks of most Southeast Asian and Thai kitchens. Although it is often served as a soup, it really has enough substance to qualify as a main course stew. I often sneak in 2 Tbsp VSOP cognac just before serving. A Thai relative taught me that breaking a green chilli or two into the soup gives it a new, fiery dimension!

Duck and Salted Vegetable Stew Tom Pak Kaat Dong Phed

Serves 6–8

Water 1.5 litres (48 fl oz / 6 cups)

Duck breasts 2, medium, fat trimmed, sliced into 8 pieces each

Pork leg 200 g (7 oz)

Salted mustard vegetable 400 g (14$^1/_3$ oz), cut into thick slices

Preserved sour plums 4

Sugar 1 tsp

Tomatoes 2, cut into halves

Light soy sauce 2 Tbsp

Brandy or cognac (optional) 2 Tbsp

Green chillies 4, coarsely chopped

1 Place water, duck and pork leg in large pot. Bring to the boil over medium heat and cook for 35 minutes.

2 Add salted mustard vegetable, sour plums, sugar, halved tomatoes and soy sauce. Cover pot and reduce heat. Simmer for 35 minutes, or until duck is tender. Skim off as much oil and impurities from the surface as possible.

3 Add brandy and green chillies. Serve hot.

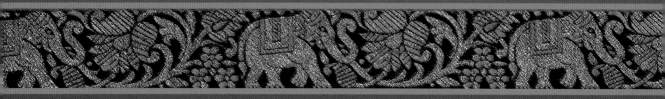

Beef, Pork and Lamb

Acknowledged as one of the most complicated curries to prepare, this recipe is believed to have come from Persia in the 16th century. It is very typical of south Thailand cooking as the region nudges north Malaysia where the population is largely Muslim. Malaysian cuisine is itself influenced heavily by early Indian, Arab and Persian traders. Perhaps it is because of the characteristic rich and spicy flavour from chillies, cumin and cardamom that this evolutionary hypothesis is more acceptable, and the reason why it is often called a Muslim curry. Certainly many Malaysian beef and mutton curries are just a whisper away from a quintessential Massaman curry.

Massaman Beef Curry Gaeng Massaman Nuea

Serves 4

Vegetable oil 2 Tbsp

Onion 1, large, peeled and finely sliced

Massaman curry paste (see page 40) 2 Tbsp

Coconut milk 500 ml (16 fl oz / 2 cups)

Fish sauce 2 Tbsp

Lime juice 2 Tbsp

Sugar 1 tsp

Beef sirloin 450 g (1 lb), cut into thin strips

Apple aubergines (brinjals/eggplants) 4, cut into halves

Sweet basil leaves 1 sprig

1 Heat oil over medium heat. Stir-fry onion for 5 minutes, or until soft. Add curry paste, coconut milk, fish sauce, lime juice and sugar. Stir well. Bring curry mixture to the boil, then reduce heat and simmer for 5 minutes.

2 Add beef and simmer for 15 minutes, or until beef is tender. Add aubergines and simmer for 5 minutes.

3 Dish out and serve immediately, garnished with basil leaves.

Southern Thai cooking draws liberally from the Malaysian-Indian styles, which in itself is a hybrid that goes back centuries. Characteristically hot, dry and redolent of spices, the Thai elements come from an infusion of palm sugar, lime juice and kaffir lime leaves. "Paneang" has become a term that is commonly associated with Thai curries, and refers to the neighbouring Malaysian island of Penang.

Dry Beef Curry Paneang Nua

Serves 4

Ground coriander 2 Tbsp

Ground cumin 2 tsp

Red curry paste (page 39) 1 Tbsp

Garlic 2 cloves, peeled and minced

Beef sirloin 450 g (1 lb), cut into thin slices

Coconut milk 300 ml (10 fl oz / 1¼ cups)

Fish sauce 2 Tbsp

Palm sugar 3 Tbsp

Kaffir lime leaves 6

Lime juice 2 Tbsp

1 Heat a wok over low heat. Dry-fry coriander and cumin until fragrant. Remove from heat. Combine with curry paste and garlic and mix well.

2 Reheat wok. Fry paste over medium heat until fragrant. Add beef slices. Stir well to coat beef slices. Stir in coconut milk and mix well.

3 Reduce heat and simmer for 10 minutes, or until oil separates from curry. Add fish sauce, palm sugar, kaffir lime leaves and lime juice and stir well.

4 Dish out and serve immediately, with steamed white rice.

Whenever pork is featured as a stir-fry, it is always better to use a cut that has some fat for better texture and flavour. The fat also adds just the right amount of moistness to the dish. This recipe has been in my family for generations and there is never any question of dumping leftovers as the pork, practically pickled after a few days, makes a delicious sandwich spread.

Stir-fried Pork with Spices Muu Phad Nam Prik Pao

Serves 8

Water 1 litre (40 fl oz / 5 cups)

Boneless rib cut of pork 1 kg (2 lb 3 oz)

Cooking oil 4 Tbsp

Palm sugar 2 Tbsp

Dark soy sauce 1 Tbsp

Fish sauce 2 Tbsp

Kaffir lime leaves 6, finely sliced

Paste

Onion 1, large, peeled and finely sliced

Garlic 4 cloves, peeled and finely chopped

Prawn (shrimp) paste 1 Tbsp

Galangal 2.5-cm (1-in) knob, peeled and finely sliced

Lemon grass 2 stalks, tough outer leaves removed and finely chopped

Dried chillies 4, soaked to soften and drained

Candlenuts 6

1 Bring water to the boil. Add pork and cook for 10 minutes, or until pork changes colour and is cooked. Remove, drain and set aside to cool. Cut pork into medium-fine slices and set aside.

2 Prepare paste. Using a mortar and pestle, pound ingredients until fine. Heat oil over medium heat. Stir-fry paste for 5 minutes, or until fragrant. Add pork slices and stir-fry for 10 minutes, or until pork is cooked.

3 Add palm sugar, dark soy sauce, fish sauce and kaffir lime leaves. Stir-fry for 5 minutes, or until gravy is almost absorbed.

4 Dish out and serve hot.

NEIL PERRY

Undisputedly one of Australia's leading lights in the dining realm, Neil's reputation has gone global over the past two decades. His passion and in-depth knowledge of Asian cuisines is no mean feat when you consider Australia was a culinary backwater a mere 25 years ago when the epitome of fine dining was to "slap a shrimp on the barbie".

This BBQ pork dish will no doubt endear itself to many for its lip-smacking succulence. It differs slightly from that which you get in a Chinese restaurant; no red food colouring is used but the results are more than satisfying. The preserved bean curd not only provides more than a hint of vermilion but also imparts an intense sweet, savoury flavour.

Barbecued Pork Muu Daeng

Serves 4

Pork neck 450 g (1 lb), cut into 4-cm (2-in) thick slices

Honey 6 Tbsp

Marinade

Preserved red bean curd 4 Tbsp

Light soy sauce 2 Tbsp

Chinese cooking wine 5 Tbsp

Salted soy beans 3 Tbsp

Hoisin sauce 4 Tbsp

Castor (superfine) sugar 4 Tbsp

Garlic 3 cloves, peeled and minced

1 Prepare marinade. Place ingredients in a blender and blend into a fine paste. Transfer paste to a large bowl.

2 Place pork to steep in the marinade for 2 hours. Set aside in a cool place.

3 Preheat oven to 240°C (464°F). Place a baking rack over a large roasting pan filled with water. Arrange pork strips on roasting pan. Brush honey over pork and roast in preheated oven for 30 minutes.

4 Remove pork from oven and leave to cool. Dish out and serve on its own or with steamed white rice.

SOMKID BHANUBANDH

Somkid may have married into royalty, but she is no slouch when it comes to pitching it with her staff. Often, she cooks up a storm for them, and this pork curry is a Thai staple that takes on regal nuances under her hands.

Although yellow curry paste is not as well known as its red and green cousins, it serves poultry and seafood very well. It is closely related to the north Malaysian style of curries, and fresh turmeric is the cornerstone ingredient. It is also delicious as a marinade for grilled chicken. Pork has total compatibility with bamboo shoots, whether fresh or canned. The wonderful thing about bamboo shoots is that they retain their crunchiness no matter how long you cook them.

Pork Curry with Bamboo Shoots Gaeng Muu Normai

Serves 8

Vegetable oil 2 Tbsp

Yellow curry paste (page 38) 2 Tbsp

Coconut milk 435 ml (14 fl oz / 1³/₄ cups)

Lean pork 400 g (14¹/₃ oz), cut into thin slices

Canned bamboo shoots 200 g (7 oz), drained and sliced

Fish sauce 2 Tbsp

Lime juice 2 Tbsp

Sugar 1 tsp

1 Heat oil over medium heat. Stir-fry curry paste for 1 minute, or until fragrant. Add coconut milk and pork. Stir-fry until pork changes colour and is cooked, then reduce heat and simmer for 10 minutes.

2 Add bamboo shoots and simmer for 10 minutes, or until gravy is thickened. Add fish sauce, lime juice and sugar and cook for another 5 minutes.

3 Dish out and serve hot, with steamed white rice.

CHIANG MAI COOKERY SCHOOL (SOMPAN NABNIAN)

This curry is a typical northern curry and one of the most popular in this neck of the woods. Although it is made using water, the final result has a thick, gravy-like consistency and according to Sompan, it reminds him of steak and kidney pudding! Perhaps being married to an English woman evokes such sentiment. It also uses young galangal (from the kitchen garden), which has a lighter and more refreshing flavour than standard or old galangal.

Northern-style Pork Curry Gaeng Ohm Muu

Serves 4

Oil 2 Tbsp

Red curry paste (see page 39) 4 Tbsp

Pork tenderloin 300 g (10¹/₂ oz), cut into thin slices

Chicken stock or water 500 ml (16 fl oz / 2¹/₂ cups)

Lemon grass 1 stalk, trimmed, use only 5-cm (2-in) from bulbous end

Young galangal 60 g (2 oz), peeled and finely sliced

Kaffir lime leaves 6, finely sliced

Fish sauce 2 Tbsp

Light soy sauce 1 Tbsp

Salt ¹/₂ tsp

Sawtooth coriander 5 leaves, coarsely chopped

Spring onion 1, cut into 2.5-cm (1-in) lengths

Coriander leaves (cilantro) a handful

1 Heat oil in a wok over medium heat. Stir-fry curry paste for 2 minutes. Add pork and stir-fry another 2 minutes.

2 Add chicken stock or water, lemon grass, galangal and kaffir lime leaves and stir well. Bring to the boil. Add fish sauce, soy sauce and salt. Reduce heat and simmer for 20 minutes, or until pork is tender.

3 Dish out and serve garnished with sawtooth coriander, spring onion and coriander leaves.

VATCHARIN BHUMICHITR

Back in the 1980s, looking for lemon grass was tantamount to seeking a needle in a haystack. Two decades on, even diehard Chinese chefs have jumped on the Thai bandwagon in using this aromatic ingredient. They give spare ribs a lovely perfume for that resounding 'sanuk' flavour, which applies to everything that gives pleasure.

Deep-fried Spare Ribs with Chilli and Lemon Grass Kraduhk Muu Thot

Serves 2-4

Pork spare ribs 450 g (1 lb), cut into 5-cm (2-in) lengths

Sesame oil 2 Tbsp

Cooking oil for deep-frying

Marinade

Garlic 2 cloves, peeled

Lemon grass 1 stalk, tough outer leaves removed

Red chillies 4

Salt $^1/_2$ tsp

Sugar 1 tsp

Ground white pepper $^1/_2$ tsp

Fish sauce 2 Tbsp

Dipping sauce

Salt 1 tsp

Ground white pepper 1 tsp

Lime juice 3 Tbsp

1 Prepare marinade. Using a mortar and pestle, pound garlic, lemon grass and chillies into a fine paste. Transfer to a large mixing bowl. Add salt, sugar, pepper and fish sauce. Mix well.

2 Place spare ribs in to steep in the marinade and set aside in a cool place for 1 hour.

3 Meanwhile, prepare dipping sauce. Combine ingredients and set aside.

4 Heat oil in a wok over medium heat. Deep-fry spare ribs until golden brown. Drain and serve immediately with dipping sauce on the side.

PHILIPPA KINGSLEY

When Philippa says she was a Thai maiden in a former life, it is not said with tongue firmly in cheek. Blonde and petite, but a dynamo of activity, she conducts classes on Thai cuisine, holds talks on Thai culture and caters to embassy parties with exotic aplomb.

The south of Thailand comes to the forefront with a fragrant array of spices that represent India, Malaysia and Thailand. This dish originated from the Malaysian Muslims who settled and blended into the tranquil setting of southern Thailand. The avocado is a fusion touch that does not detract one iota from the intrinsic flavour of the Massaman paste.

Massaman Curry of Lamb with Avocado and Lemon Grass
Gaeng Massaman Gae

Serves 4

Baby potatoes 450 g (1 lb), peeled

Coconut milk 750 ml (24 fl oz / 3 cups)

Massaman curry paste (page 40) 2 Tbsp

Boneless leg of lamb 1.5 kg (3 lb 4^1/$_2$ oz), excess fat trimmed, diced into 2.5-cm (1-in) thick slices

Pearl onions 250 g (9 oz), small, peeled

Lemon grass 5 stalks, trimmed, use only 5-cm (2-in) from bulbous end

Fish sauce 3 Tbsp

Lemon juice 250 ml (8 fl oz / 1 cup)

Palm sugar or brown sugar 2 Tbsp

Unsalted roasted peanuts 140 g (5 oz)

Ripe avocados 2, peeled and sliced

1 Leave potatoes unpeeled, if desired. Alternatively, peel and carve for a decorative effect.

2 Heat a wok over high heat. Add 3 Tbsp coconut milk and curry paste and stir-fry for 4 minutes, or until fragrant.

3 Add lamb and stir well to coat evenly. Reduce heat and cook for 10 minutes. Remove from heat and set aside.

4 Prepare a large, heavy-bottomed saucepan. Heat remaining coconut milk over low heat and bring to a slow boil. Add lamb and simmer for 25 minutes.

5 Add potatoes, onions, lemon grass, fish sauce, lemon juice and palm or brown sugar and cook for 20 minutes, stirring occasionally.

6 Cover saucepan and simmer for 30 minutes, or until potatoes and lamb are tender. Add peanuts and cook for 10 minutes.

7 Transfer lamb curry to a serving dish and arrange avocado slices as desired. Serve immediately.

KHUN SUNANT WILIARAT (MADAM PA)

This stalwart of the Blue Elephant in London has really earned her laurels as the undisputed queen of Thai curries. Otherwise known affectionately as Madam Pa, Sunant was embraced to the bosom of the Thai royal family for her exquisite creations.

Vegetables temper the powerful spiciness of this twist to simply-prepared Thai curry that is very more-ish. Although lamb is not generally featured in Thai dishes, it is cooked most often by northerners. Traditionally, goat meat or mutton is used in this region.

Chillied Lamb Gae Phad Prik

Serves 2

Spanish onion 1, large, peeled and finely sliced

Red chillies 2, finely chopped

Garlic 2 cloves, peeled and finely chopped

Red curry paste (page 39) 1 tsp

Vegetable oil 3 Tbsp

Boneless leg of lamb 150 g (5¹/₃ oz), cut into 2.5-cm (1-in) thick slices

Apple aubergine (eggplant/brinjal) 1, cut into quarters

Pea aubergines (eggplants/brinjals) 5

Green, yellow and red capsicums (bell peppers) 1 each, small, cored, seeded and cut into thin slices

Coconut milk 2 Tbsp

Water 3 Tbsp

Green peppercorns 1 Tbsp

Sugar 1 tsp

Fish sauce 1 Tbsp

Light soy sauce 2 tsp

Sweet basil leaves 1 sprig

Coriander (cilantro) leaves a handful

1 Combine onion, chillies, garlic and curry paste in a mortar. Pound mixture into a fine paste.

2 Heat oil in a wok over medium heat. Stir-fry paste until fragrant. Add lamb and stir-fry for 2 minutes. Add aubergines and capsicums. Stir-fry for 2 minutes, or until just tender.

3 Add coconut milk, water, peppercorns, sugar, fish sauce and light soy sauce and stir well. Add basil leaves and stir-fry for another 2 minutes.

4 Dish out and serve hot, garnished with coriander leaves.

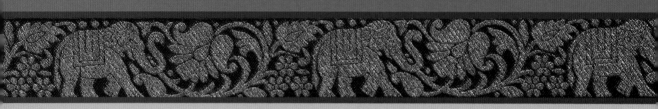

Fish and Seafood

DAVID THOMPSON

Not too long ago, fusion food did not earn much cachet; it was even sniffed at for being a little too outré and even nonsensical. David prefers to call it modern Australian, apropos much of what we find today in European and Pacific Rim countries that did not have any claim to ancient culinary heritage. David continues to research Thai culinary techniques and recipes, giving them his personal rubber stamp.

This is a 'sour' gaeng krua, given an extra dimension with palm sugar and tamarind water. To balance this extra seasoning, the curry paste includes coriander root and kaffir lime zest. Coconut cream, by definition, is richer and thicker than normal coconut milk and has the consistency of double or clotted cream.

Mussel and Mangosteen Curry Gaeng Hoi Maleng Pu Makrut

Serves 2

Mussels 300 g (10¹/₂ oz)

Coconut cream 350 ml (14 fl oz / 1³/₄ cups)

Coconut milk 125 ml (4 fl oz/ ¹/₂ cup)

Palm sugar 2 Tbsp

Fish sauce 1 Tbsp

Tamarind juice 1 Tbsp paste, mixed with 250 ml (8 fl oz / 1 cup) and strained

Mangosteens 3, peeled

Salt 1 tsp

Kaffir lime leaves, 3, shredded

Curry paste

Smoked trout 1, small

Dried chillies 8, seeded and soaked to soften and drained

Galangal 2.5-cm (1-in) knob, peeled and finely chopped

Lemon grass 4 stalks, tough outer leaves removed and finely chopped

Coriander leaves (cilantro) and root 2 sprigs, finely chopped

Red shallots 3, peeled and finely chopped

Garlic 3 cloves, peeled and finely chopped

Prawn (shrimp) paste 1 Tbsp

1 Soak mussels in a large basin of water for 30 minutes to expel any dirt and sand. Remove mussels carefully, being careful not to agitate sand at the bottom of the basin. Scrub mussels clean under a running tap. Drain and set aside.

2 Prepare curry paste. Preheat oven to 220°C (440°F). Grill trout for 5–7 minutes. Remove from oven and set aside to cool. Use a spoon to scrape flesh off skin and mash lightly to break fish up further. Set aside.

3 Combine chillies, galangal, lemon grass, coriander, shallots and garlic in a mortar. Pound ingredients until fine. Transfer to a blender and add prawn paste and minced fish. Blend into a fine paste.

4 Bring coconut cream to the boil over medium heat. Add 3 Tbsp paste and fry until fragrant. Gradually add coconut milk and stir well. Add palm sugar, fish sauce and tamarind juice and cook for 1 minute.

5 Add mangosteen flesh and mussels. Reduce heat and allow to simmer for 8 minutes. Discard any unopened mussels.

6 Season with salt and stir well. Serve immediately, garnished with kaffir lime leaves.

I particularly love this treatment of mussels with ginger, coriander and pepper as a great stir-fry. It is particularly delicious when you can throw table manners to the wind and dip in with your fingers; that is the only real way to enjoy mussels.

Stir-fried Mussels in Ginger Sauce Hoi Maleng Pu Phad Khing

Serves 4

Mussels 2 kg (4 lb 6 oz)

Cooking oil 4 Tbsp

Ginger 5-cm (2-in) knob, peeled and minced

Garlic 2 cloves, peeled and minced

Coriander leaves (cilantro) and root 2 sprigs, root bruised and finely chopped

Ground black pepper 1 tsp

Lime juice 3 Tbsp

Fish sauce 2 Tbsp

Chinese cooking wine 125 ml (4 fl oz / $^1/_2$ cup)

Water 250 ml (8 fl oz / 1 cup)

Sweet basil leaves 1 sprig

Red chilli 1, seeded and cut into strips

1 Prepare mussels (page 149).

2 Heat oil in a wok over high heat. Stir-fry ginger and garlic for 1 minute, or until fragrant, Add coriander and stir-fry for 1 minute. Add mussels, pepper, lime juice and fish sauce. Stir-fry for 2 minutes.

3 Add cooking wine and water. Cover wok, reduce to low heat and simmer for 8 minutes. Discard any unopened mussels.

4 Serve immediately, garnished with sweet basil leaves and red chilli strips.

KHUN SUNANT WILIARAT (MADAM PA)

Madam Pa's talent for the spice is not by any means limited to only meat cookery. Seafood, especially shellfish, under her hands are transformed from being merely briny denizens to dishes fit for royalty.

When she throws in the herbs and spices, Madam Pa brooks no compromise for the subtle fire of chillies to wrap around these deep-fried prawns. And she says you can do this in all of five minutes.

Prawns with Red Curry Sauce Chuchi Gung

Serves 2

Dried prawns (shrimps) 1 Tbsp

Oil for deep-frying

Prawns 8, peeled and deveined, leaving heads and tails intact

Vegetable oil 1^1/$_2$ Tbsp

Red curry paste (see page 39) 3 Tbsp

Coconut milk 180 ml (6 fl oz / ^{3}/$_4$ cup)

Sugar 2 Tbsp

Fish sauce 1 Tbsp

Kaffir lime leaf 1, finely shredded

Assorted salad greens a handful

Chinese cabbage 1 small head, finely shredded

Coconut cream 2 Tbsp

Coriander leaves (cilantro) a handful, finely chopped

Sweet basil leaves 2 sprigs

1 Using a mortar and pestle, pound dried prawns until fine. Set aside.

2 Heat oil for deep-frying in a wok over high heat. Deep-fry prawns for 3–5 minutes, or until prawns change colour and are cooked. Remove, drain and set aside.

3 Heat vegetable oil over low heat. Fry red curry paste for 2 minutes. Add coconut milk and stir well. Bring to the boil for 1 minute. Add dried prawns, sugar, fish sauce and kaffir lime leaf. Stir well, remove from heat and set aside.

4 Arrange prawns on a bed of salad greens and Chinese cabbage. Drizzle red curry sauce over prawns, followed by coconut cream.

5 Dish out and serve garnished with basil leaves.

NEIL PERRY

Together with his compatriot David Thompson, Neil is responsible for putting the new Australian cuisine on the world map, culling from many Thai and Asian influences that have re-written Australian cuisine from its former British heritage that was resolutely in the "meat and two veg" camp.

This is a classic Thai dish that received some rich compliments when I served it to my guests at a lunch. The flavours blend extremely well and the aromatic sauce can also be teamed with fish fillets, poured over or served on the side. If you cannot find coconut vinegar, sometimes known as palm vinegar and a favourite condiment in the Philippines and Thailand, use rice vinegar instead.

Five-flavoured Prawns Gung Thot Ha Rot

Serves 4

Coriander leaves (cilantro) 5, finely chopped

Mint leaves 5, finely chopped

Vegetable oil 750 ml (24 fl oz / 3 cups)

King prawns 450 g (1 lb)

Tapioca (cassava) flour 1 Tbsp

Dipping sauce

Tamarind juice 2 Tbsp paste, mixed with 250 ml (8 fl oz / 1 cup) water and strained

Coconut vinegar 1 tsp

Fish sauce 1 Tbsp

Sugar 1 Tbsp

Finely ground dried chillies $1/2$ tsp

Roasted sesame seeds 1 tsp

Deep-fried shallots 2 Tbsp

Deep-fried garlic 2 Tbsp

1　Place coriander and mint leaves in oil and set aside.

2　Prepare dipping sauce. Place tamarind juice, vinegar, fish sauce and sugar in a small pot. Cook mixture over medium heat until slightly thickened. Add chillies, sesame seeds, shallots and garlic. Stir well, remove from heat and set aside.

3　Using a sharp knife, make a small incision on underside of each prawn. Leave shell intact.

4　Coat prawns in tapioca flour. Heat vegetable oil over high heat. Fry prawns until crisp and golden brown. Drain well.

5　Serve prawns immediately, with dipping sauce on the side.

There are few ingredients that can match the sweet succulence of fresh prawns, and when battered and fried to a golden brown, then bathed in an aromatic sweet and sour sauce, they are ambrosial. This batter is a personal favourite as cream crackers make for crunchiness that lasts and lasts.

Sweet and Sour Prawns Peaw Wan Gung

Serves 4

Cream crackers 8

Tiger prawns 8, peeled and deveined,
  leaving tails intact

Egg 1, beaten

Oil for deep-frying

Basic sweet and sour sauce (page 44)

1 Using a mortar and pestle, pound cream crackers until fine. Coat prawns in egg, then coat with ground cream crackers.

2 Heat oil in a wok over medium heat. Deep-fry prawns until crisp and golden brown. Remove from heat and drain.

3 Serve prawns immediately, with sweet and sour sauce on the side.

This is extremely easy to prepare even for the utmost novice. It is a very aromatic dish as a starter or entrée. Fresh tiger prawns are best for this dish, but if you have access only to frozen prawns, seek out those that are frozen individually rather than in a block— it simply means you get to extract what you need without having to defrost the entire lot.

Prawns with Lemon Grass Pla Gung

Serves 4

Lime juice 2 Tbsp

Fish sauce 2 Tbsp

Chilli powder 1 tsp

Palm sugar 1 Tbsp

Water 125 ml (4 fl oz / $^1/_2$ cup)

Prawns 400 g (14$^1/_3$ oz), peeled and deveined. leaving tails intact

Lemon grass 1 stalk, tough outer leaves removed and finely sliced

Shallots 3, peeled and finely sliced

Ginger 1-cm ($^1/_2$ -in) knob, peeled and finely sliced

Chicory lettuce 1 small head, leaves separated

Kaffir lime leaves 2, finely sliced

1 Combine lime juice, fish sauce, chilli powder, palm sugar and water. Bring to the boil over medium heat for 2 minutes.

2 Add prawns and cook for 2 minutes, or until prawns change colour and are cooked.

3 Add lemon grass, shallots and ginger. Cook for another 2 minutes.

4 Arrange lettuce on a serving dish and place prawns on top. Serve garnished with kaffir lime leaves.

TYM SRISAWATT

As a past mistress at vegetarian and northern Thai dishes and not one to compromise, Tym is relentless when it comes to seeking out unusual ingredients for her award-winning recipes. This grilled prawn dish is exquisitely spicy and aromatic and makes a marvellous barbecue dish for entertaining al fresco. *The best prawns to use are uncooked tiger prawns that may cost a little more, but are supremely delicious.*

Grilled Spiced Prawns Gung Phao

Serves 4

Red chillies 3, finely chopped

Kaffir lime leaves 2, finely chopped

Garlic 2 cloves, peeled and finely chopped

Ground turmeric 1 tsp

Sugar 1 tsp

Cooking oil 2 Tbsp

Tiger prawns (shrimps) 16

1. Place chillies, kaffir lime leaves and garlic in a mortar and pound into a fine paste. Transfer to a mixing bowl. Add turmeric, sugar and oil, mix well and set aside.

2. Prepare prawns. Trim feelers. Using a sharp knife and leaving prawn shells intact, create small pockets by making a medium-deep incision down the length of each prawn.

3. Spoon paste into prawn pockets. Set aside to marinate for 10 minutes.

4. Cook prawns over a barbecue grill, or in a preheated oven at 180°C (350°F) for 8 minutes, until prawns change colour and are cooked.

KEN HOM

Another ingenious invention on Ken's part, this simple dish of prawns may not be classical Thai but it more than passes muster for its beautiful flavour. Coriander and ginger come from the Thai camp and rice wine and sesame oil are resoundingly Chinese. Together, they make beautiful culinary music.

Grilled Prawns with Fresh Coriander, Vinegar and Ginger Sauce
Gung Phao Phad Pak Chee Khing

Serves 2–4

Light soy sauce 1 Tbsp

Rice wine or dry sherry 1 tsp

Sesame oil 1 tsp

Prawns (shrimps) 450 g (1 lb), peeled and deveined, leaving tails intact

Dipping sauce

Coriander leaves (cilantro) 2 Tbsp, chopped

Rice vinegar 2 tsp

Ginger 1-cm ($^1/_2$-in) knob, peeled and finely chopped

1 Combine soy sauce, rice wine or dry sherry and sesame oil in a mixing bowl. Mix well. Place prawns in to marinate for 10 minutes.

2 Combine ingredients for dipping sauce and set aside.

3 Arrange prawns on a baking tray. Cook in a preheated oven at 180°C (350°F) for 10 minutes, turning prawns over once every 3–4 minutes.

4 Serve prawns hot, with dipping sauce on the side.

SOMKID BHANUBANDH

Mottled crabs come mainly from the Indian Ocean. They are seasonal, but are now available frozen. Much smaller than Dungeness crabs or other cold Atlantic crustaceans, they have a delicate sweetness. Uncooked, they are a grey-green colour with specks of white and turn completely deep pink when cooked.

Deep-fried Spicy Stuffed Crab Puu Cha

Serves 4

Mottled crabs 4

Ground black pepper 1 tsp

Palm sugar 1 tsp, ground

Lime juice 1 Tbsp

Ground cumin 1 tsp

Fish sauce 1 Tbsp

Prawns 150 g (5^1/$_3$ oz), finely minced

Minced chicken 55 g (2 oz)

Spring onions (scallions) 2, finely chopped

Eggs 2, beaten

Corn flour (cornstarch) 1 Tbsp

Cooking oil for deep-frying

Coriander leaves (cilantro)

1 If crabs are alive, place in the freezer for a few hours. Remove and scrub crabs clean. Remove triangular flap on the underside of each crab, then pull top shell off. Remove gill filaments and rinse crabs. Separate pincers and legs from crab.

2 Place crabs in boiling water for 5 minutes, or until crabs change colour and are cooked. Remove, drain and leave to cool.

3 Extract meat from crab, including the tomalley. Clean and reserve empty crab shells.

4 Place pepper, palm sugar, lime juice, cumin and fish sauce in a mixing bowl. Mix well. Add crabmeat, prawns, chicken and spring onions and mix well to marinate. Add eggs and corn flour mixture and mix well.

5 Spoon filling into crab shells. Heat oil in a wok over medium heat. Deep-fry for 5 minutes, or until stuffed crabs are crisp and golden brown. Remove and drain.

6 Serve crabs garnished with coriander leaves, a wedge of lime and chilli sauce, or Prawn Paste with Lime Leaf (page 45) as a dipping sauce on the side, if desired.

TYM SRISAWATT

When Tym decided to decamp to Eastbourne after running her south London establishment, it was something of a challenge to the taste buds of punters not known to venture very far beyond fish and chips. After two years, patrons have been resolutely converted to Tym's spicy creations, such as this classic.

Generally deemed an appetiser, Hor Mog Thalay comes with a lot of panache, and is really good enough to be served as a main course offering, especially when served in its own banana leaf wrapping, au naturel. Hor Mog Thalay can also be baked or cooked on a charcoal grill for barbecues.

Spiced Steamed Fish in Banana Leaf Hor Mog Thalay

Serves 4

Mackerel or cod fillets 450 g (1 lb)

Fish sauce 2 Tbsp

Lime juice 2 Tbsp

Sugar 1 tsp

Eggs 2, beaten

Coconut milk 4 Tbsp

Banana leaves 4

Paste

Ginger 2.5-cm (1-in) knob, peeled and finely chopped

Red chillies 2, finely chopped

Ground turmeric 1 tsp

Onion 1, large, peeled and finely chopped

Lemon grass 2 stalks, tough outer leaves removed and finely chopped

Ground coriander 1 Tbsp

Prawn (shrimp) paste 1 tsp

1 Using a spoon, scrape meat off fillets and mash lightly to break meat up further.

2 Combine minced fish with paste ingredients in a blender and blend into a fine paste. Transfer to a mixing bowl. Add fish sauce, lime juice, sugar, eggs and coconut milk. Mix until well blended.

3 Bring a pot of water to the boil. Blanch banana leaves for 1 minute to make them more pliable. Remove, drain and cut into 15 x 15-cm (6 x 6-in) squares.

4 Spoon 2 Tbsp fish paste into the centre of each banana leaf square. Fold 2 opposite sides of leaf over paste, then turn up the corners of 1 side of the leaf and press together with your index finger and thumb. Tuck in the other corners, forming a triangular peak. Secure parcel with a toothpick. Repeat steps for remaining banana leaf squares.

5 Steam parcels over high heat for 10 minutes. Fish paste is cooked when an inserted toothpick comes out clean. Serve immediately.

Tip: As an alternative way of serving, spoon fish paste into lightly oiled ramekins, cover with foil and steam over high heat for 15 minutes.

Another Thai hybrid rich with Chinese elements, this recipe produces the best results when you buy fresh, meaty fish. Garoupa meat is particularly sweet, but snapper and even mullet can be cooked in the same way. Somehow, I cannot feel the same frisson of excitement when faced with fish fillets cooked thus–for me, it has to be the whole fish, head, tail and all. Besides, the meat on the cheeks of large fish has a delicate taste and texture. Adjust the amount of chillies according to taste.

Ginger Fish Pla Khing

Serves 4

Garoupa 1, about 1.5 kg (3 lb 4¹/₂ oz), cleaned and gutted

Corn flour (cornstarch) 3 Tbsp

Oil for deep-frying

Vegetable oil 2 Tbsp

Garlic 4 cloves, peeled and finely chopped

Lemon grass 2 stalks, tough outer leaves removed and finely sliced

Ginger 5-cm (2-in) knob, peeled and finely sliced

Preserved yellow bean sauce 2 Tbsp

Red chillies 4, finely sliced

Chinese mushrooms 6, stems removed, soaked to soften and cut into thin slices

Spring onions (scallions) 3 stalks, cut into 5-cm (2-in) lengths

Lime juice 2 Tbsp

Sugar 1 Tbsp

Fish sauce 2 Tbsp

Water 250 ml (8 fl oz / 1 cup)

Coriander leaves (cilantro) a handful

1 Using a sharp knife, score 2 cuts across fish diagonally. Coat well with 2 Tbsp corn flour.

2 Heat oil for deep-frying over high heat. Deep-fry fish until golden brown and crisp. Remove and set aside to drain. Place on a serving plate.

3 Heat vegetable oil over medium heat. Stir-fry garlic, lemon grass and ginger for 2 minutes, or until fragrant. Add yellow bean sauce, chillies, mushrooms and spring onions. Stir-fry for 2 minutes.

4 Add lime juice, sugar, fish sauce and remaining corn flour mixed with water. Mix well and simmer for 2 minutes, or until sauce has thickened.

5 Drizzle sauce over fish and serve garnished with coriander leaves.

NEIL PERRY

If there is one thing that Australia is known for, it is seafood; among the freshest from unpolluted waters. How Neil coaxes the most endearing flavours from fish is a culinary wonder and his insistence on the best produce has seen him win a slew of awards.

Red Emperor Fish is a snapper with attitude and it takes on a divine flavour from the marriage of soy sauce, coriander and ginger. The Thai method of steaming fish is very similar to the Chinese ginger and shallot method, but with a bit more spice. Again, this recipe suits any delicate white-fleshed whole fish.

Steamed Red Emperor Fish in Soy and Oyster Sauce
Pla Neung Nam See Yiew Phad Nam Man Hoy

Serves 4

Red emperor (or any white-fleshed fish) 900 g
(2 lb), scaled, gutted and cleaned

Coriander roots (cilantro) 2, bruised and chopped

Ginger 2.5-cm (1-in) knob, peeled and sliced
into thin strips

Red chillies 2, large, seeded and cut into
thin strips

Green bird's eye chillies 3, seeded and
finely chopped

Sugar 1 tsp

Ground white pepper $^1/_2$ tsp

Shallots 3, peeled and finely sliced

Seasoning

Chicken stock 85 ml ($2^1/_2$ fl oz / $^1/_3$ cup)

Light soy sauce 2 Tbsp

Oyster sauce 3 Tbsp

1   Use paper towels to pat fish dry. Using a sharp knife, score both sides of fish with criss-cross cuts.

2   Steam fish over high heat for 10–12 minutes, or until fish is slightly undercooked.

3   Add seasoning ingredients, coriander roots, ginger, chillies, sugar and pepper. Continue steaming for another 5 minutes. Fish is cooked when flesh turns opaque and flakes off easily from the bones when poked with a fork. Remove fish and transfer to a serving platter. Reserve steaming liquid.

4   Pour steaming juices over fish and garnish with sliced shallots. Serve immediately.

Running through my grandparents' fruit plantation was a little river where often lurked small catfish that appeared to have come from a delta that spread out into a larger river. My cousins and I would trawl the shallow waters with nets and scoop a dozen or so each time. We would bear them with triumph to the kitchen where mother would gut and clean them before making this delicious tamarind curry.

Tamarind Catfish Curry Gaeng Pla Duk Makarm

Serves 4

Catfish fillets (or red snapper or monkfish) 450 g
(1 lb), sliced

Salt 1 Tbsp

Vegetable oil 3 Tbsp

Tamarind juice 2 Tbsp paste, mixed with
500 ml (16 fl oz / 2 cups) and strained

Sugar 1 tsp

Fish sauce 1 Tbsp

Lime juice 1 Tbsp

Paste

Lemon grass 2 stalks, trimmed, use only
5-cm (2-in) from bulbous end

**Yellow or red curry paste
(pages 38 and 39)** 1 Tbsp

Kaffir lime leaves 4

1 Rub catfish slices with salt and set aside.

2 Prepare paste. Place all ingredients in a blender and blend into a fine paste. Heat oil in a wok over medium heat. Fry paste for 2 minutes, or until fragrant.

3 Add tamarind juice, sugar, fish sauce and lime juice and stir well. Add catfish slices, reduce heat and simmer for 12 minutes, or until fish is cooked.

4 Dish out and serve hot.

I often use trout for this dish, especially the boneless fillets. This fish has more flavour than we accord it, is available all year round and is ideal for deep-frying. Trout can be slippery to handle because of its slimy skin. To counter this, rub a little salt all over to cleanse the slime.

Deep-fried Fish with Nam Prik Sauce Pla Tod Nam Prik

Serves 4

Corn flour (cornstarch) 4 Tbsp

Salt 1 tsp

Ground black pepper 1 tsp

Trout fillets 4

Oil for deep-frying

Cucumber 1, peeled and finely sliced

Nam Prik sauce

Fish sauce 4 Tbsp

Lime juice 2 Tbsp

Palm sugar 1 Tbsp

Ginger 2.5-cm (1-in) knob, peeled and minced

Finely chopped bird's eye chillies 1 Tbsp

Warm water 2 Tbsp

1 Prepare Nam Prik sauce. Combine all ingredients in a blender and blend into a fine paste. Set aside.

2 Combine corn flour, salt and pepper in a mixing bowl and sprinkle over trout, coating evenly.

3 Heat oil in a wok over medium heat. Deep-fry trout until crispy and golden brown. Remove and drain before serving.

4 Place on a serving plate and serve trout with cucumber slices and Nam Prik sauce on the side.

Desserts

Bananas in coconut milk is one of the simplest Thai desserts, and yet a true classic that transcends all levels of dining. You will find it at the humblest street stall and also within the ranks of royal Thai cooking, the difference being only in its mode of presentation. It takes mere minutes to prepare and lifts the common banana to sublime heights of flavour. You may use just-ripe bananas or even plantains, but large cooking bananas hold their shape better despite being less flavoursome and sweet. The coconut sauce can be used for any soft tropical fruit such as jackfruit, durians and mangoes.

Bananas in Coconut Milk and Palm Sugar Kluay Buah Chee

Serves 4

Large ripe bananas 8, peeled
Coconut milk 500 ml (16 fl oz / 2 cups)
Palm sugar 3 Tbsp
White sugar 1 Tbsp
Screwpine (*toei*) leaves 2, knotted

1 Slice bananas into 4 pieces each. Discard any part of the banana that is dark brown and mushy.

2 Combine coconut milk, sugars and screwpine leaves in a pot. Bring to a gentle boil over medium heat. Stir constantly until palm sugar is completely dissolved.

3 Add bananas and cook for 3 minutes before removing from heat.

4 Serve bananas warm or chilled.

This is poetry in delectable taste, a most interesting dessert that has crunch, sweetness and bejeweled presence. "Tup tim" means "rubies" in Thai. When cooked, each droplet of the water chestnut coated with tapioca flour does resemble this precious gem. Water chestnuts are commonly found in cans, but fresh ones are occasionally available. These are covered with a dark skin and are fiddly to prepare, but have more flavour.

Red Rubies Tup Tim Krob

Serves 4

Water chestnuts 250 g (8 oz), peeled

Red food colouring 2 tsp

Tapioca (cassava) flour 100 g (3^1/$_2$ oz)

Iced water 1 litre (32 fl oz / 4 cups)

Crushed ice enough for 4 portions

Coconut syrup

Water 180 ml (6 fl oz / ^{3}/$_4$ cup)

Sugar 100 g (3^1/$_2$ oz)

Coconut milk 300 ml (10 fl oz / 1^1/$_4$ cups)

1 Cut water chestnuts into small cubes. Place in a mixing bowl and add food colouring. Mix well to colour each piece evenly. Add tapioca flour and coat water chestnut pieces.

2 Bring a pot of water to the boil. Add water chestnut cubes and boil for 4 minutes, or until water chestnut cubes float to the surface. Remove, drain and immediately plunge into iced water to set the flour coating on water chestnut cubes. Drain and set aside.

3 Prepare coconut syrup. Bring water and sugar to the boil over medium heat until sugar is dissolved. Add coconut milk, stir well and remove from heat. Set aside to cool.

4 Spoon water chestnut cubes over crushed ice in bowls and drizzle with coconut syrup.

Tip: Enhance this dessert with cubes of mango and halved lychees for a rainbow-hued touch.

Probably the most high profile of all Thai desserts, glutinous or sticky rice allows one to ring the changes with other fruit like durian, jackfruit or bananas. At first glance, it looks like an unlikely combination, but the sweetness of mangoes marries with savoury coconut rice in the most lip-smacking way.

Sticky Rice and Mangoes Khao Niaw Mamuang

Serves 2

Glutinous (sticky) rice 150 g (5$^1/_3$ oz),
  washed and soaked for 4 hours

Coconut milk 300 ml (10 fl oz/1$^1/_4$ cups)

Sugar 1 Tbsp

Salt $^1/_2$ tsp

Ripe Thai mangoes 2, large, peeled
  and seeded

Coconut cream 2 Tbsp

1 Place glutinous rice in rice cooker or steaming bowl. Add just enough water to cover rice.

2 Combine coconut milk, sugar and salt and mix well. Pour over rice and mix well. Steam rice for 30 minutes, or until liquid is completely absorbed. Leave rice to cool. Shape cooled glutinous rice into small mounds.

3 Slice mangoes into large chunks and place alongside glutinous rice. Serve warm or cool, with coconut cream drizzled over rice.

In the corner of my grandparents' beloved vegetable patch grew a clump of tapioca, a root that is extremely forgiving of unforgiving soil. We would pluck the tender young leaves for curries and haul out the large, brown-skinned roots for making this family favourite. This is something of a hybrid dessert, a blend of Thai and Singapore elements that is always trotted out for afternoon snacks. It tastes equally good baked or steamed.

Baked Tapioca Cake Khanom Saku

Serves 6

Tapioca (cassava) root 900 g (2 lb), peeled

Palm sugar 300 g (10^1/$_2$ oz)

Water 4 Tbsp

Sugar 100 g (3^1/$_2$ oz)

Coconut milk 300 ml (10 fl oz / 1^1/$_4$ cups)

Desiccated coconut 4 Tbsp

1 Cut tapioca into small pieces. Using a blender, blend tapioca until fine. Remove and place in a colander. Drain out as much juice as possible by pressing hard on the tapioca. Set aside.

2 Melt palm sugar in a pot over medium heat. Add water and sugar and stir well to blend. Strain to remove any hard lumps, if necessary.

3 Combine tapioca, syrup and remaining ingredients in a mixing bowl. Mix well. Pour into a lightly oiled 20 x 5-cm (8 x 2-in) square or round baking dish. Bake in a preheated oven at 250°C (475°F) for 30 minutes.

4 Reduce temperature to 200°C (400°F) and bake for another 30 minutes, or until top of tapioca cake is golden brown.

5 Remove from oven and set aside until just warm before cutting into desired serving shapes.

The traditional Thai version uses half of a small pumpkin or a wedge of a larger one, as a container for the custard. You can also use any type of sweet squash to steam the custard, but using an ordinary shallow steaming dish will do as well.

Steamed Coconut and Egg Custard Sangkhaya

Serves 4

Eggs 5

Coconut milk 300 ml (10 fl oz / 1¹/₄ cups)

Sugar 280 g (10 oz)

Salt ¹/₂ tsp

Vanilla essence ¹/₂ tsp

Muslin cloth 30 x 30-cm (12 x 12-in) square

Screwpine (*toei*) leaves 2, knotted

Vanilla ice cream 4 scoops

1 Break eggs into a mixing bowl. Add coconut milk and sugar and mix until well blended. Add salt and vanilla essence and mix well. Strain mixture through muslin cloth to remove any lumps.

2 Place screwpine leaves in a steaming dish and pour mixture over. Steam, covered, over medium heat for 30–40 minutes, or until custard has set. Set aside to cool.

3 Meanwhile, place ice cream into 4 serving glasses. Leave in the freezer until custard is ready.

4 Cut custard into small cubes and divide among serving glasses on top of ice cream. Garnish as desired and serve immediately.

BLUE ELEPHANT COOKERY SCHOOL (RUNGSAN MULIJAN [CHANG])

The concept of running a cookery school adjoining its eponymous restaurant did not take shape until the 1980s, the late venerated Ken Lo breaking ground with his Belgravia Memories of China. Even so, cookery schools devoted to Asian cuisine are thin on the ground here in the UK. In Thailand, however, they are of very high profile, the Blue Elephant being a relative "Johnny-come-lately".

I still salivate over Chang's creations that I wolfed down when I made a flying visit. This hybrid Mango Cheesecake is to die for; a scented and sainted blend of tropical fruit and fromage. Cashew nuts make a good substitute, if one has allergies to walnuts.

Mango Cheesecake Khanom Cake Nei Mamuang

Serves 8

Cheesecake base

Cream crackers 100 g (3¹⁄₂ oz)

Walnuts 1 Tbsp

Milk 2 Tbsp

Unsalted butter 55 g (2 oz)

Cheesecake mixture

Cream cheese 350 g (12 oz)

Sugar 100 g (3¹⁄₂ oz)

Egg yolks 2

Mango 1, large, peeled, seeded and finely mashed

Lime juice 2 Tbsp

Topping

Sugar 30 g (1 oz)

Sour cream 150 g (5¹⁄₃ oz)

Mango 1, small, peeled, seeded and finely mashed

Sliced almonds 4 Tbsp, roasted

1 Prepare cheesecake base. Using a mortar and pestle, pound cream crackers and walnuts until fine. Add milk and mix well.

2 Lightly grease a 20 x 5-cm (8 x 2-in) round baking dish with butter. Pack in cracker and walnut mixture firmly.

3 Prepare cheesecake mixture. Using a whisk or electric mixer, combine cream cheese, sugar and egg yolks until well blended. Add mango and lime juice and whisk to combine. Pour over cheesecake base and spread out evenly. Place in a preheated oven at 170°C (330°F) for 25–30 minutes. Cake is ready when an inserted toothpick comes out clean.

4 Meanwhile, prepare topping. Using a whisk or electric mixer, combine sugar, sour cream and mango until well blended.

5 Remove cheesecake from oven. Spread topping over cheesecake and return to the oven. Bake for another 10–15 minutes, or until topping is firm, then remove and leave to cool completely. Place in refrigerator to chill for an hour.

6 Top with almond slices and serve.

This has the most interesting etymology. Once upon a time, a Chinese herbal brew made from boiling a type of bark was believed to have efficacious powers. It transcended the apothecary to the home and became a favourite cooling drink. The Chinese call it "Fairy Grass" in reference to the immortality of mythical Chinese sprites. It is a mainstream item in all Chinese and Thai grocers and comes in canned form. In colour, grass jelly ranges from dark green to almost black; basically, it is a herbal jelly of yin, or cooling properties reflecting the yin and yang tenet of universal harmony.

Grass Jelly Chow Guay

Serves 4

Grass jelly 650 g (1 lb 7 oz)

Water 1 litre (32 fl oz / 4 cups)

Screwpine (*toei*) leaves 4, knotted

Sugar 200 g (7 oz)

Crushed ice (optional)

1 Cut grass jelly into 2.5 x 2.5-cm (1 x 1-in) cubes. Keep refrigerated until needed.

2 Bring water to the boil. Add sugar and screwpine leaves and boil until sugar is completely dissolved. Discard screwpine leaves and leave syrup to cool. Strain sugar syrup before refrigerating to chill.

3 Prepare 4 serving glasses. Spoon some grass jelly into each glass and pour chilled sugar syrup over. Add crushed ice, if desired, before serving.

This is a delicate, if somewhat fiddly, dessert to make but absolutely delicious. You will find that making the screwpine (toei) cups requires some dexterity (and patience!) but what price should one pay for culinary perfection? Royal Thai cuisine probably spawned this as the ladies of the court had the time to indulge in such cuisine arte. Tradition demands that the dessert be so contained because of the fragrance imparted by the leaf. Take the easy way out and steam them in small ramekins or cups, but dot each with tiny squares of screwpine leaves or rose petals. It is a rather more elaborate version of Coconut Cups (page 196), with the added crunch of water chestnuts.

Water Chestnut Coconut Cups Tako Haew

Serves 4

Screwpine leaf cups

Screwpine (*toei*) leaves 14

Fine bamboo slivers or toothpicks 14

Bottom layer

Screwpine (*toei*) leaves 2

Cold water 500 ml (16 fl oz / 2 cups)

Corn flour (cornstarch) or rice flour
150 g (5^1/$_3$ oz)

Arrowroot flour 1 Tbsp

Sugar 200 g (7 oz)

Fresh water chestnuts 100 g (3^1/$_2$ oz), peeled
and finely chopped

Top layer

Coconut cream 300 ml (10 fl oz / 1^1/$_4$ cups)

Salt ^{1}/$_2$ tsp

Rice flour 2 Tbsp

1 Prepare screwpine leaf cups. Blanch leaves in boiling water for 1 minute to make them more pliable. Cut into 20-cm (8-in) lengths. Fold leaf at every 4-cm (1.5-in) interval.

2 Use a pair of scissors to make 4 small incisions on one side of each leaf, up to the central vein of each leaf, using the folded lines as a guide. Trim edge of leaf, on cut side, a little. Shape each leaf into a square cup with interlocking folds. Secure leaf cups with bamboo slivers and set aside.

3 Prepare bottom layer. Using a mortar and pestle, pound screwpine leaves to extract essence. Squeeze leaves to extract as much juice as possible. Strain liquid into a mixing bowl.

4 Add water, corn flour, arrowroot flour and sugar and mix until well blended. Bring to a gentle simmer over low heat. Add water chestnuts and stir until liquid becomes translucent. Spoon into screwpine leaf cups until half full and set aside to cool.

5 Prepare top layer. Combine ingredients in a clean saucepan and bring to the boil for 2–3 minutes, or until thickened. Spoon into screwpine leaf cups over bottom layer. Refrigerate to chill.

6 Serve garnished with rose petals, if desired.

DAVID THOMPSON

Some 25 years when I ate a delicious meal at David's Thai outlet in Sydney's Darley Street, he had already impressed with his unique gift for lighting the touchpaper of the cuisine to create some memorable classics. Over the decades, this inspired chef has recorded them all for posterity in his award-wining tome "Thai Food", recognised as a definitive of the cuisine. His influence on Thai cooking was recognised by the Thai government. They consulted him at the Suan Dusit Institute in Bangkok.

Here the interplay of sweet syrup and sour fruit is enhanced with the nutty and crunchy character of deep-fried shallots. Rambutans are apricot-sized fruits with hairy red skin, indigenous to most of tropical Asia. The flesh is sweet, succulent and faintly reminiscent of firm lychees. They are also available in canned form in Asian and Thai supermarkets.

Green Mango with Rambutans Som Chum

Serves 2-4

Rambutans 20, peeled and seeded

Green mango 1, small, peeled, seeded and
   cut into thin strips

Crushed ice 450 g (1 lb)

Deep-fried shallots 3 Tbsp

Syrup

Sugar 250 g (8 oz)

Water 500 ml (16 fl oz / 2 cups)

Screwpine (*toei*) leaf 1, knotted

Salt $^1/_2$ tsp

1   Prepare syrup. Combine ingredients in a saucepan and bring to the boil over medium heat. Stir constantly, until sugar and salt are completely dissolved. Discard screwpine leaf and leave to cool completely.

2   Divide crushed ice into 4 serving bowls. Combine rambutans and mango and spoon over ice. Pour syrup over and serve garnished with deep-fried shallots. Shallots may also be served on the side, if desired.

*This two-tiered pudding, common in many parts of Southeast Asia, is a gentle, aromatic after-meal dessert. Using arrowroot as a thickening base gives a light and translucent finish. The Thai version usually uses screwpine (*toei*) leaf colouring and essence for the bottom layer.*

Coconut Cups Khanom Thuey

Serves 4

Bottom layer

Screwpine (*toei*) leaves 2, finely chopped

Water 90 ml (3 fl oz / $^3/_8$ cup)

Rice flour 200 g (7 oz)

Arrowroot or tapioca (cassava) flour 2 Tbsp

Coconut milk 450 ml (18 fl oz / $2^1/_4$ cups)

Palm sugar 4 Tbsp

Top layer

Coconut milk 300 ml (10 fl oz / $1^1/_4$ cups)

Rice flour 3 Tbsp

Salt a pinch

1 Prepare bottom layer. Using a mortar and pestle, pound screwpine leaves. Add 3 Tbsp water and squeeze pounded leaves to extract as much juice as possible. Strain liquid into a mixing bowl.

2 Add rice flour, arrowroot flour and half of coconut milk to screwpine leaf juice. Mix well. Add remaining coconut milk, mix well and set aside.

3 Melt palm sugar in a pot over medium heat. Add remaining water and stir constantly, until palm sugar is completely dissolved. Remove from heat and add to coconut milk and flour mixture. Mix well, then pour evenly into 4 ramekins or heatproof serving cups.

4 Steam over medium heat for 20 minutes and set aside to cool. Refrigerate to set.

5 Prepare top layer. Combine ingredients and mix well. Spoon into ramekins on top of chilled bottom layer, then leave to chill in the refrigerator before serving.

Index